The Thirty-nine Articles:
Buried Alive?

The Anglican Articles of Religion
and the Case for Confessional Christianity

Samuel C. Pascoe

CB ♦ ♦ BO

First Printing.
LATIMER PRESS
P.O. Box 391657
Solon, OH 44139

ISBN 1-893051-00-5

To Order: 1-800-248-5058

This book is dedicated to my family, to my lovely and longsuffering wife, Beth, whose patient endurance and wise encouragement made it possible for me to endure to the end; to my children, Samuel, David and Jonathan who missed their dad while he holed up at various times to finish.

I also dedicate this book to the staff of Grace Church (especially Frances and Tammy, my two right hands without whom much would have been left undone), and the people of Grace Church for giving me the gift of time and for their vision for the larger Church of which they are a part.

I also wish to acknowledge the deep debt I owe to the following people: To my mentor and friend, the Rev. Dr. William Stafford (Academic Dean at Virginia Theological Seminary) whose love for our Lord's Church is surpassed only by his love for our Lord. He may disagree with some of my conclusions but he will also find that he gave me the gift of an inquiring and discerning heart.

To the U.S. Marine's greatest contribution to Anglican theology, the Very Rev. Dr. John Rodgers, the retired but far from retiring Dean Emeritus of Trinity Episcopal School for Ministry whose devotion to the Articles and whose passion for Grace and Truth often inspired me. I am a pastor, not a scholar. If this book fulfills its purpose, it will whet your appetite to learn more about the Articles. If so, you can do no better than to read Dr. Rodgers' authoritative book on the subject, available from Trinity Seminary in Ambridge, PA.

To the Rev. Drs. Steve Brown and Luder Whitlock (both of Reformed Theological Seminary) and the Rt. Rev. John W. Howe (Bishop of Central Florida) who once said to me: "You ought to write a book."

To my dear friends Neil, Marcia, Peter and Mary for making me say cheese when I whined and for bucking me up when I was about to buckle under.

To the Bishop Payne Library at my alma mater, Virginia Theological Seminary, for allowing me to plant myself in their far too comfortable oak seats, dust off some neglected volumes from their splendid stacks, and to immerse myself in the wonderful history of this magnificent mastodon called Anglicanism.

Table of Contents

⋄ *Introduction* ⋄

Once the layman was anxious to hide the fact that he believed so much less than the vicar: he now tends to hide the fact that he believes so much more. Missionary to the priests of one's own church is an embarrassing role; though I have a horrid feeling that if such a mission work is not undertaken the future history of the Church of England is likely to be short.

C. S. Lewis

Though only 26 years of age, King Josiah had been on the throne of Judah for 18 years.[1] The socio-political structures he inherited were in chaos. The reign of his grandfather, King Manasseh, was described as "evil" and full of "detestable practices." His father, King Amon, had been assassinated after an equally corrupt reign of only two years. The challenges facing King Josiah were pervasive. His kingdom was in disarray, his people were in despair, and the Temple, that magnificent symbol of the Lord's presence and favor, was in disrepair.

Josiah, his advisors, and lieutenants acted wisely and well. By the end of the second decade of his regency, his kingdom had been restored to a sound political and economic base. It was now time to restore the temple. As the work was drawing to a close, Hilkiah the high priest found a copy of the "Book of the Law" and gave it to Shaphan, the king's secretary. He, in turn, took it to the king. In a narrative, remarkable for its understatement, Shaphan reported to the king about paying the temple craftsmen and then, almost as an afterthought, mentioned how Hilkiah had found the dusty, neglected book.

On hearing the words of the book, King Josiah was thunderstruck. He tore his cloak. He ordered prayers for discernment. He called for a time of repentance and renewal.

---

1 This story is found in II Kings 21 and following.

The story of the restoration under King Josiah is one of the most remarkable and heartening stories in all of Scripture. But there are two other remarkable stories here. First, how is it that so great a document, so seminal a truth, should have been lost and neglected? Was there a dark, deliberate conspiracy to hide these previously well-known truths from the people? Was there a moment when a decision was made to divorce this document from the worshiping life of the community? Probably not. It is more likely that the story of their neglect followed the all-too-human pattern of gradual disregard, a slow, almost imperceptible drift into self-destruction.

The second, even more remarkable, thing is that the worship continued without knowledge of the covenant law. How was it possible for the temple, with its worship, its culture, and its priesthood, to continue to function for all those years without any knowledge of the covenant law?

While no one would equate the Anglican Articles of Religion[2] with the covenant law of Israel, we neglect them at our peril. It is my conviction that if our church and its people understood the implications of overlooking this covenant document, there would be a similar outcry followed by a similar renewal of faith and commitment.

This should not surprise us because, from the beginning, they have been an important part of the life of the Protestant Episcopal Church in America. If the Episcopal Church is to respond wisely, effectively and faithfully to these challenges, the Articles must be honored, protected, and presented as a worthy and necessary starting point for pastoral, theological, and ecclesiastical dialogue.

The ecumenical creeds of the church (which are identified and affirmed in Article VIII) are the foundation of our common understanding of The Faith. The various confessions presuppose creeds and build on them. Creeds are short ("Jesus is Lord" is perhaps, the earliest of all Christian creeds, and many would say the only one truly needful). Creeds can be used liturgically,

---

2   The Articles can be found in the back of *The Book of Common Prayer* (American, 1979) beginning on page 867.

focus on the Godhead, creation, redemption and are drawn up to convey The Faith to novices or inquirers. Confessions are longer, not suitable for liturgical use, focus on anthropology, soteriology (*the study of salvation*), polity, pneumatology (*the study of the Holy Spirit*), convictions about the nature and use of the scriptures, and are used as tests for the orthodoxy of those who seek the high calling of being a "teacher" or "elder." "*Not many of you should presume to be teachers, my brothers, because you know that we who teach will be judged more strictly*" (*James 3:1*).

This caution about more strict judgement is one of the main reasons why some form of subscription to doctrinal articles should be required of those who accept the call to a position of leadership within the church. Even though "subscription" (in the form of the baptismal vows) to the Apostles' Creed is all that is required of members, those who seek or receive a different calling within the Body must conform to a "higher" or "more definitive" standard.

One of the Apostle Paul's last bits of advice to his young protégé, Timothy, contains a prescription and a promise: "*Watch your life and doctrine closely. Persevere in them, because if you do, you will save both yourself and your hearers*" (*I Timothy 4:16*). Because we have neglected the prescription, we are in peril of losing the promise.

Not too long ago, I met a young woman who was transferring into the church I serve from another Episcopal congregation. During the course of our conversation, she told me that the reason she chose to join the Episcopal Church was because she "could believe anything she wanted to and still be a good Episcopalian." After further conversation, it turned out this young woman (who had been an Episcopalian for many years) would actually have felt more at home in a Buddhist Temple. Her clear impression, after years of attending Episcopal Churches, was that what one believes is not really an issue in the Episcopal Church. She became an Episcopalian to get away from theology.

Soon after that conversation, a gentleman who was quite involved in our church and on the vestry, told me that the reason he left the Methodist Church and became an Episcopalian was his abhorrence of any notion of God's providence in matters of salvation. He had fled Methodism, he said, to get away from it. Unlike my lady friend above, this kind soul was at least a Christian in his basic beliefs. But somewhere along the line, the lines had blurred. He was enjoying the trip, but he was on the wrong bus. Unlike the young woman, theology was important to him, but what the Episcopal Church believes was so obscured for him that he found himself involved in a form of involuntary hypocrisy. When I told him that the Episcopal Church has, at least historically, affirmed both the benevolence and the reality of God's providence in matters of salvation, he was flummoxed.

These two conversations confirmed my conviction that Episcopalians need to renew their commitment to what has been called "The English Protestant Creed," the Articles of Religion.

In 1864, Bishop John Henry Newman wrote *Apologia Pro Vita Sua*, a reasoned defense of his decision to leave the Anglican Church to join the Roman Church. It was more autobiographical than polemical. He answered his critics by telling his story. We will learn more about him and his story later. This book is about one chapter in the story of the Anglican Church. It is also a chapter in the author's life as well.

This book is a kind of *Apologia Pro Vita Sua* for me for it was because of the Articles of Religion that I claimed the Anglican Church as my home. But it is also a *Apologia Pro Vitis Suis* (a reasoned defense for our common life as a communion) because if it were not for the Articles, there would not have been an Anglican Church to join. It is an attempt to explain why the Anglican Communion exists from a *theological* perspective. This is because unless a church or communion can articulate a theological reason for its existence, its existence cannot be justified. Without primary reference to God (*theos*) as He has revealed Himself as The Word (*logos*) revealed in the words of Scripture, a church is simply one of many noble but purely temporal and temporary volunteer associations. Without reference to theology, personal preferences as regards style, worship, polity, etc. become only self-serving prejudices at best, idols at worst.

Anglicans usually offer their *raison d'être* in terms of historical/apostolic continuity, or in the power and majesty of the liturgy, or in terms of a rather intriguing series of historical "accidents" (in the "oops" sense) that were "accidental" (in the Aristotelean sense) to the substance of The Faith. Is there a core doctrine of Anglicanism, a unique theological stance that is not only compelling but is also congenial to history AND the contemporary situation? There is. And the most compelling *raison d'être* of Anglicanism is found in a remarkable document called the Articles of Religion.

These clear, concise articulations of the Anglican Faith have guided and guarded the Anglican Church for over 400 years. In addition to the Episcopal Church, USA, the Anglican Churches in England, Ireland, Wales, Scotland, Australia, New Zealand, Canada, South Africa, West Africa, Uganda, and Japan are committed to their authority. But they find themselves increasingly relegated to the back of the bus. It is the burden of this book to show that if the Anglican Communion (at least in its European and American manifestations) is ever going to recapture the vision, vigor and vitality that is its birthright, it must rediscover and reaffirm these wise and winsome articulations of a living Christianity.

Speaking of birthrights, the affirmation that one is a "cradle Episcopalian" is usually greeted by warm smiles, nodding heads, and a comfortable sigh of recognition and approval. On the other hand, when one identifies oneself as a "creedal Episcopalian," brows furrow, eyebrows arch, and a sense of disease, distrust, and distress settles upon the group. A "creedal Episcopalian?" Who, or what, is that? We can understand someone who is an Anglican because they were born to it. But what do we do with someone who chooses to be an Anglican because he or she consents to its theology and believes that this communion has rightly discerned and described the Christian experience?

Being an Anglican is a matter of belief, not breeding. The life of common prayer and liturgy which nourishes us and sustains us finds its own strength in a common core of theological conviction, a right understanding of Who God is and who He calls us to be. This core doctrine of the Episcopal Church is found in and founded in the Articles.

It has been observed that what separates a river from a swamp is the presence of definable boundaries. By depositing the Articles in the basement of the *BCP*, the Episcopal Church has taken a giant step into a swamp. While it may be true that their position within the covers of the *BCP* has changed, their status as the defining document of Anglican theology has not changed. Yet, this sort of subtle slip-sliding away is all-too-often the way Anglicans seem to do theology. We are too polite to have a rousing, and potentially divisive, doctrinal debate. So we ease our theology gently out the backdoor, like unwelcome guests at our party, all the while assuring them that they really are our dear friends, and, won't they come again when they can't stay so long, and please to be careful on the way home, etc. . . .

Who is writing?

Because I think it helpful when an author is forthcoming with his or her personal convictions and perspectives, I will offer mine now.

I joined the Episcopal Church in 1981 and was ordained a presbyter/priest in 1985. I am the rector of a middle-size church in a middle-size suburb of a middle-size American city. In other words, I am a working priest — not an antiquarian academic who longs for the "good old days." The parish church I serve is growing and alive with young families and creative, cutting edge programs. In a recent year we had 53 baptisms and only three funerals. This book is not a plea for a sentimental journey to a bygone era when iron men went to sea in wooden ships. It is an attempt to articulate a case for an articulated Faith.

I chose to enter the Anglican Communion after a decade of work with a para-church ministry put me in contact with many denominations. Because I am also an Evangelical (see glossary) by conviction, the historic integrity and world-wide impact of Anglican Evangelicalism has always meant a great deal to me. It is in that soil that my faith took root and grew. It is out of that heritage that I now write. It is that strong and vibrant fellowship I seek to strengthen.

Having said that, I am also aware that the Anglican Church consciously and conscientiously casts a broad net. No one theological perspective (not even "broad-churchmanship") can comprehend it all. Yet, just as the body is the sum of its parts, so also The Church is the sum of its parts. And, in the wise words of St. Paul, the hand cannot say to the foot, "I have no need of you." It is my conviction that, at this time in our history, The Church is in danger of saying to its confessional, evangelical members: "We have no need of you. In fact, we're not sure you ever belonged with us. Get thee gone." This book is my attempt to address that unfortunate, and self-destructive, impulse.

To Whom Am I Writing?

This book is intended to be read by thoughtful Christians who want to understand the Anglican approach to Christianity. It will be helpful

- for those "outside" the communion who want to know more about what Anglicans believe,

- for those inside the communion who have despaired because they believe that the Anglican Church does not offer clarity of conviction,

- for study groups in churches that want to deepen their understanding of their heritage,

- for clergypersons who somehow missed some of these truths during their seminary training, and

- for anyone who wants to understand how faithful people have wrestled in real times and in real places with the real issues of how to be a Christian in this world.

As I write, I am conscious of all of these groups. I think of my friends in the community for whom liturgical, hierarchical Protestantism is oxymoronic. I think of the many men and women who have joined our parish family, or who grew up in other Anglican parishes, but who still do not understand that our distinctives are more substantial than a lovely building or a wonderful nursery. I think of groups of faithful people who are weary of getting together to share prejudices and/or ignorance. I think of seminary-trained colleagues who were trained to listen care-

fully to the saints in the pews tell their story but who are virtually unaware of the story of the saints who now compose the
cloud of witnesses.

And I think especially of a group of people in our church
whose self-effacing name, *NERDS* (for "No Easy Reading & Discussion Society"), belies their intense, honest, and noble desire
to have a simple faith that is not simplistic and to love God with
their minds as well as their hearts, souls and strength.

If you see yourself in any of these little mirrors, this book is
for you.

You have gathered, then, that I am a "professional" Anglican, in all senses of that provocative term. It has been God's grace
to me that I am able to earn my livelihood by engaging in a vocation (literally my "calling") which accords with those things
that I most sincerely "profess." In this most noble sense, then, all
Christian people are professional Christians, for it is Christ Whom
we profess.

If that is what it means to be a professional Christian, what
can it mean to be a "confessional" Christian?

Discussion Questions _____

1) Can a person be both a cradle *and* creedal Christian? Is
   there a difference?

2) How did you come to faith in Christ? Was a it a gradual
   process or sudden event?

3) How has your church home helped or hindered that
   process and/or event?

4) Have you ever changed denominational affiliation? If so,
   why?

ങ O · N · E ﻉ

The Present Necessity: The Case for Confessional Christianity and an "Articulated" Anglicanism

James Kelly, a writer in Washington DC, doesn't believe in God, the resurrection, miracles, or any of it. He is neither a Christian nor a theist, but he is a very happy Episcopalian, a member of St. Mark's on Capitol Hill where he has taught Sunday School and served on the vestry. He took a poll of parishioners and discovered there are many more like him. According to this news story, "The least satisfied members were the few who hold any traditional Christian beliefs. It is the orthodox who are the heretics."
Quoted from *First Things*, Vol. 78. Dec. '97, p. 77

W e live in a world that is both fascinated by "spirituality" and suspicious (or downright contemptuous) of spiritual authority — at least when that authority takes an ecclesiastical or institutional form. The naive assumption seems to be that the transcendent is an equal opportunity realm. Because it is available to all it must, therefore, also be equally apprehendable and comprehendable by all. People who would not set foot in a National Park or even a shopping mall without a guide (human or written) will set off into the realm of the spiritual without so much as a finger to the wind. The spiritual landscape of the late 20th century is marked by a bewildering cacophony of theophanies. The old paradigms aren't worth a dime anymore. Even the word paradigm is already out of date.

1

As the 20th century draws to a close, Christianity faces a situation not unlike the one it faced at the beginning of the 16th century. As that distant century dawned, new technologies and discoveries were challenging old assumptions and methods. Spiritual authority, which had for so long been fixed and focused, was up for grabs in the *zeitgeist* (the "spirit of the age") which had been ushered in by the Renaissance. New political and cultural alliances were being forged. A whole "new world" was opening across the Atlantic ocean, and a "new England" was being explored and settled. The 16th century was alive with new insights and new possibilities.

The catalog of characters whose intellectual, artistic, and spiritual innovations defined the time reads like a Who's Who of History: Shakespeare (1564-1616), Michelangelo (1474-1564), da Vinci (1452-1519), Brahe (1546-1601), Kepler (1571-1630), Galileo (1564-1642), Erasmus (1466-1536), Thomas More (1478-1535), Luther (1483-1546), Calvin (1509-1564), and Cranmer (1489-1556) to name just a few. Perhaps no age so mirrors our own as this one.[3] As new allegiances and alliances are forged in the crucible of real life lived in a real world, it is necessary to stop long enough to take our bearings and to mark our path. In the 16th century, when the written word was just becoming widely available through the printing press, and when people cared about ideas, to consciously break with one's tradition without giving a well-thought out rationale would have been, well, unthinkable. It was an era when people placed a high value on propositional truth.

The people of God have always been called upon to be able to verbally articulate their faith. From the powerful *Shema Israel* of Deuteronomy 6, to the simple New Testament creed of "Jesus is Lord," to the intricacies of the Athanasian Creed, people of faith have always sought to put words to their convictions. This is wise and helpful for at least three reasons:

(A)   It helps the believer and the believing community to think through their faith when it actually has to be put into words.

---

3   Barbara Tuchman's masterpiece *A Distant Mirror* is must reading for any serious student of contemporary culture.

(B)   It makes the experience of faith somewhat "transferable" in the sense that others can hear about what God has done in the past (or is doing in the present) and use such expressions to guide their own prayers and/or reflections on what God is doing in their lives.

(C)   Because creeds cannot say everything, the mere exercise of creating and/or reciting a creedal formula helps the believing community to focus on those issues that really are important.

At the Reformation, the then emerging churches which rejected the Roman allegiance defined their doctrinal position in formal "Confessions." ("Confession" in the New Testament denotes public adherence to the truth of Jesus Christ. See, for example, *I Timothy 6:13; Matthew 10:32; Phil. 2:11; I John 4:2ff.*) Paragraphs of these Confessions were called "heads" (*capita* or what we would call "chapters") or "articles" (*articuli*—literally "parts" or "points").[4] The Anglican Articles of Religion grow out of this *milieu*.

Having said that, honesty compels us to begin by facing the fact that there is a widespread suspicion (it doesn't quite qualify as a "conviction" because few people seem to care enough to be "convicted" one way or the other) that the Articles are simply pre-Enlightenment, pre-Revolutionary, and pre-critical baggage. Historian A. G. Dickens speaks for many when he calls the Articles a "rather heavy clutter of anachronisms" for which there "remains a lingering, superstitious reverence."[5] As a result, they were buried in the back of the *BCP*.

One reason may be that our basic theological temperament has changed over the years. As one scholar pointed out, "The reason that has contributed most to the decay in the estimation of the Articles in modern Anglicanism has been the recent rejection of propositional revelation."[6]

---

4   Packer, J. I., *A Guide to the 39 Articles Today*, p. 6.

5   Dickens, A. G., *The English Reformation*, p. 252.

6   Knox, David Broughton, "The Position of the Thirty Nine Articles. . .," p. 7.

"Propositional revelation" means that "God reveals himself to men through meaningful statements and concepts expressed in words."[7] In 1968, the Archbishop's Commission on Christian Doctrine said, "the Articles belong to a period of trust in propositional revelation. Nowadays, many theologians tend to see revelation in situational, existential, and personal, rather than propositional terms."[8] But to even make such observations is to impugn a theological bias where none exists. The Articles themselves mandate no particular view of revelation. The Commission's recommendation prompted J. I. Packer to observe: "Now this is nonsense, worthy perhaps of drunken sailors but hardly sober bishops."[9]

Even if we grant that all truth is not propositional truth, is propositional truth "untrue" because it is propositional? The subjective, "existential truth" of experiencing the Hallelujah chorus began with mastering the simple, objective, "propositional" truth of hitting the right keys on the piano. Jesus often thought and expressed Himself propositionally (e.g., *"God is spirit and those who worship him must worship in spirit and in truth." John 4:24*), Paul often thought and expressed himself propositionally (e.g. *"God is not a God of disorder but of peace" (I Corinthians 14:33)*.

From the simplest prayer to the most magnificent hymns, the Christian Faith is communicated propositionally. "Jesus loves me, this I know, for the Bible tells me so." "God is great. God is good. And we thank Him for our food." "A mighty fortress is our God, a bulwark never failing." "Immortal, invisible, God only wise . . ." "Jesus is Lord." "God is love." Even the rather intelligent sounding theological postulate, "The language of God is silence," is itself a propositional statement.

The people who populate our pews think propositionally. Neither a doctor nor a carpenter serves his or her discipline well

---

7   Knox, p. 70. (Knox's book contains a helpful discussion about propositional vs. non-propositional views of revelation.)

8   "Report of the Archbishop's Commission on Christian Doctrine," *Subscription and Assent to the Thirty-nine Articles*, p. 35.

9   Packer, J. I., *The Thirty-nine Articles*, p. 24.

when he or she denigrates propositional truth. The old adage *"Measure twice; cut once"* applies with equal urgency to both neuro-surgeons and nail-bangers. If our church is to have credibility in the contemporary intellectual *agora* where our people live and work, if the church is going to have any hope of communicating to men and women for whom (naive as it may be) the only truth is propositional truth, we must be able to "articulate" our faith. By definition, that requires "articles."

Speaking of propositions, 77% of Episcopalians believe the proposition that "Jesus Christ was fully human and fully divine."[10] Should we rejoice or weep that only three out of four people in the pews believe the central fact of our Faith? While three-quarters agreed with the proposition, "My religious faith is the most important influence in my life,"[11] barely a third said that they even consult the Bible "to arrive at God's will in such areas as abortion, divorce, and human sexuality."[12] Four out of 10 Episcopalians did not agree with the proposition, "I believe in the full authority of the Bible."[13] Maybe a renewed focus on propositional truth would serve us well because somewhere along the line, these brothers and sisters have missed out on some of our core convictions.

Such indifference to theology should not surprise us. For example, in 1994, the Episcopal Church dropped the *"filioque* clause"[14] from the Nicene Creed. This is a matter of great theological importance for the church's views of God (theology), the Son (Christology), how we are brought into a relationship with God the Father (soteriology), how the Holy Spirit relates to believers, and how He related to the Son (pneumatology). Yet, when this fact was reported to the leaders of our diocese, it was prefaced with a flip disclaimer about its inconsequence and, not sur-

---

10 The Gallup Organization, Inc., "Report on The Spiritual Health of the Episcopal Church," p.13.

11 Ibid., p. 24.

12 Ibid.

13 Ibid., p. 25.

14 The *filioque* clause is that phrase in the Nicene Creed which states that the Holy Spirit proceeds from the Father *"and the Son."*

prisingly, received with laughter. It is as if the leadership of our church was saying, "Why is the church worrying about such trivial things as the theology of the Nicene Creed?" Of course, phrased in that way, no self-respecting Christian would have owned up to such indifference, but that was the clear message. The Triennial of the Episcopal Church Women got 20 minutes on the agenda; the Nicene Creed got 20 seconds. "This, then, is our situation," wrote theologian J. I. Packer, "The Church of England has fallen back into the kind of doctrinal chaos which the Articles were intended to eliminate."[15]

Over three decades ago, Anglican church historian Dr. Geoffrey Bromiley lamented the lackluster status of the Articles when he wrote: "The current neglect or evasion or even defiance of the Articles is one of the greatest tragedies of modern Anglicanism."[16] Then, in 1971 (the 400th anniversary of the final acceptance of the Articles) he recalled *A Curious Anniversary*:

> Having for many years relegated the Articles to an obscure place in small print in the Prayer Book, this church has in this anniversary year brought out an experimental liturgy from which the Articles are omitted altogether. Perhaps this is at least honest, for what many of the clergy and people know about the Articles seems to be infinitesimal.[17]

Although it conveys a deeply spiritual truth, Anglicanism's unofficial article of faith, *Lex Orandi—Lex Credendi* ("the law of praying is the law of believing"), has often become a one-edged sword, and a rather dull one at that. We are in danger of losing sight of the fact that prayer is the fruit, not the root, of belief.

It is true that I discover more of who you are by talking with you, but how I talk with you is governed and guided by what I know and believe about you. Both our Lord and His brother reminded us that it is possible to pray wrongly. All prayer is not Anglican, or even Christian. Our heritage of "common" prayer is not derived from simply sharing a common place or a common

---

15   Packer, *The Thirty-nine Articles, Their Place and Use Today*, p. 12.

16   Bromiley, quoted by Toon, "The English Protestant Creed," p. 153.

17   Bromiley, Geoffrey, "A Curious Anniversary," pp. 5-7.

form, but from our common beliefs. The Creeds and the Liturgy of the Word are important parts of both the Daily Offices and Holy Eucharist, and they always precede the prayers.

Discussion Questions

1) What forms of non-Christian "spirituality" have you encountered in the society in which you live? What could be a thoughtful Christian response to the proliferation of such earnest but often misguided yearnings for spiritual wholeness?

2) Do you share society's perceived discomfort with "propositional" truth? Why or why not?

3) The phrase "without regard for race, creed, or religion" has become an important part of the Western ethos. How can Christians honor the noble and egalitarian intent of that dictum and still be people who unashamedly embrace a creed?

4) *Lex Orandi—Lex Credendi* ("the law of praying is the law of believing") is a time-honored Anglican principle. How has your prayer life changed your theological understanding? Is the law of praying the *only* law of believing? Assuming that it is not, what might be some others?

∝ T · W · O ∾

A Brief History of
The Articles of Religion

A change in theological teaching involves either the commission or the confession of sin; it is either the profession or renunciation of erroneous doctrine, and if it does not succeed in proving the fact of past guilt, it, ipso facto, *implies present.*

John Newman, *Tract XC*

The story of the nativity of the Anglican Communion is eclipsed in its intrigue and drama[18] only by the nativity of our Lord. It has been the subject of many excellent books — and some less than excellent ones — as well as movies and drama. Even the most uninterested and under-informed Anglicans know (or think they know) the role Henry VIII played in breaking with the Church of Rome in the middle of the 16th century. Initially, the reforms of the English Church were driven as much by concerns about *real politik* as they were by concerns about the *real presence*.

Henry VIII had chosen Thomas Cranmer, a man of virtually no parish experience, to be his Archbishop of Canterbury. Henry VIII was married to Catherine of Aragon, through whom he had been unable to produce a male heir. It was thought at the time that no great nation, especially England, could be ruled by a woman. (Queen Elizabeth would prove them quite wrong within a generation.) Henry VIII sought an annulment from the Pope.

---

18 For further reading on the history of the English Reformation, the reader is urged to read, mark, learn and inwardly digest *Our Anglican Heritage* by Bishop John W. Howe, *The Protestant Face of Anglicanism* by Paul Zahl, *Thomas Cranmer: A Life* by Diarmaid MacCulloch and *The English Reformation* by A. G. Dickens.

For a variety of fascinating reasons, none was forthcoming. Young Thomas Cranmer endeared himself to Henry by coming to his sovereign's aid in this rather delicate situation. By suggesting that the King refer his connubial conundrum to the scholars of the day rather than simply to ecclesiastical jurisdiction, Cranmer showed himself to be a man who was open to new ideas — and a man who knew which way the wind blew: scholastically, politically, and ecclesiastically.

To make a long and interesting story short and much less interesting, in 1534 Henry decided to reassert control over the English Church, thus reclaiming the power that England had ceded to the Pope in 664 at the Synod of Whitby. Now severed from its Roman "head," the body of the English Church was in danger of thrashing about and doing great damage. King Henry knew he needed to exercise strong leadership and he did. While it is unlikely he thought he was "reforming" the church, that was indeed the process he had begun.

"Reformation" is a word many of us take for granted but it presumes something important. It presumes not only that the church had a discernable "form," but also that there existed a "form," either real or conceptualized, to which the "reformers" wanted to return. It was clear that the church had a form but where had it come from? The New Testament is actually fairly silent when it comes to ecclesiology. Except for a few references to the qualifications for elders and deacons, the rest is largely silence.

For the first three centuries of church history, the church was often persecuted and illicit. Then, rather abruptly, the church was catapulted into respectability by Constantine. As the church expanded into Europe, it took on different shapes as it moved westward in space and forward in time. In the 11th century, the Western Church was virtually cut off from its brothers and sisters in the east. Later, as a result of the Crusades, western intellectual life was turned upside down by the infusion of Aristotelean categories from contact with scholars in Asia.

By the time of the Protestant Reformation, nation states (a fairly new and powerful way of doing politics), the printing press (a new and powerful way of disseminating information), and the beginnings of the scientific revolution (a new a powerful way of viewing the world), were all crowding onto the stage of history. It was a very complicated time, and the church of the middle ages was not up to the task.

By the middle of the 16th century, virtually everyone agreed that the visible church was sorely in need of reform. Within the first half of that century, dozens of councils were convened throughout Europe to try to figure out how to cope with the changing world in which the church was supposed to represent the unchanging Christ.

At the time of the Reformation, the church had been formed over more than a dozen centuries through the potent, and often unpredictable, interaction of God's sovereign Spirit and human folly and frailty. Now Cranmer and his colleagues were tasked with re-forming it within a matter of a few years.

The reformers were in a situation comparable to that faced by the Israelites when they left Egypt after 400 years. The only model for government they had was the Egyptian model. They were going to be recreating a society on the move. It was comparable to trying to rebuild a car's engine and remodel the body while barreling down the highway. Could a cleric from Cambridge fill the sandals of Moses by leading the people to a renewed understanding of Who God is and what He requires of them?

Once the decision to break with Rome was made, reformation in England (the verb) proceeded toward Reformation (the noun) on three fronts: canon law, liturgy, and theology.[19] Thomas Cranmer was in a position to lead and he did. His facility with the English language (just coming into its own as a medium of worthy expression — e.g., Shakespeare 1564-1616), and his ability to turn theological discourse into a memorable turn-of-phrase, cannot be over-estimated. More subtle even than his poetic prose was his ability to use law and liturgy as servants of theology.

Cranmer's initial focus, at least publically, was on canon law. The revision of canon law was an inevitable and necessary out-

---

19 MacCulloch, Diarmaid, *Thomas Cranmer: A Life* , p. 500.

Martin Luther
1483 — 1546

come of the break with Rome. Hoping that the process of setting legal boundaries would produce a stable and orderly transition, Cranmer threw himself into the effort. He hoped the process would be ecumenical and irenic, but by 1552 the revision was proving to be neither. Part of the problem was that, whatever his merits as a canon lawyer, Cranmer was primarily motivated by liturgical and theological designs. Even his work on canon law had an overt rather than a covert theological agenda. Medieval canon law was a complex and bureaucratic paean to the magesterium, not the *mysterium tremendum*. Cranmer knew that geographical and jurisdictional boundaries were not the only boundaries that needed to be clarified in the wake of the Reformation. "Unusually for a document which sought to codify law, it also sought to lay down the boundaries of doctrine in the Church . . ."[20]

However hard it may be to change canon law, changing liturgy is even more problematic. If late 20th century American Anglicans are tempted to think revising a 50 year-old Prayer Book was tough, Cranmer had inherited a vast, cumbersome and outdated medieval liturgy that made the canons look positively streamlined.

Cranmer found what every clergyperson already knows: changing liturgy is contentious and tough because it deals most directly with the affections and habits of the heart. In this day and age, when most people know nothing of canon law and care even less, it is hard to understand the medieval mind-set which had produced generation after generation of canon fathers and sons (never mothers and daughters!). At heart Cranmer was a pragmatist, not an ideologue. He, therefore, set about to amend that which was most amenable: the theology of the church.

His attempts to reform the theology of the Church of England were guided by three factors: his ongoing dialogues with Lutheran divines, his ability to communicate theology in the context of liturgy, and his desire to see that the theology which was implicit in his liturgy be made explicit in a set of confessional articles.

---

20 MacCulloch, p. 502.

Effecting the Augsburg Affect

"The Confession of Augsburg was by far the most important document of the Reformation, and has attained a permanent position and value."[21] Cranmer had been quite taken with the style and substance of the Continental Reformers, especially with the work done in the German Church by the Lutherans. "When Henry [VIII] died in 1547, Cranmer, who had long been convinced that on all questions except eucharistic presence the Lutheran position was both biblical and patristic, set himself to re-cast the entire outward form of the Church of England in a reformed mold. Aided by a team of talented theologians, he compiled in quick succession a volume of standard evangelical sermons (the Homilies, 1547); a new Prayer Book and Ordinal (1549 and 1550 respectively; both revised in 1552); a code of canons (1552); and, last but not least, the Forty-two Articles of 1553."[22]

But Cranmer had to step gently and he knew it. As recently as 1536, Henry VIII's chancellor Thomas More had hunted down the pioneering English Bible scholar and translator, William Tyndale (b. 1492). The long arm of English ecclesiastical/civil law found him in Antwerp in 1535. There, in exile, he was burned at the stake for the anti-papal and anti-institutional act of translating the Bible into English. Cranmer knew quite well that the stakes in this high-stakes game often came with fire at the foot.

The Augsburg Confession seemed a perfect place to start. It was no flame-throwing diatribe against the ancient church. In fact, the confession had been dubbed by Luther himself as "a softly stepping apology," and he lamented its leniency on matters of purgatory, the worship of saints, and the nature of the papacy.[23]

"The whole Confession, or 'Apology,' as Melanchthon called it, is eloquent of its author's yearning to promote the reunion of divided Christendom; it breathes the spirit of defense, not defi-

21   Thomas, W. H. Griffith, *The Principles of Theology*, p. xxx.

22   Packer, *The Thirty-nine Articles*, p. 33.

23   Curtis, William A., *A History of Creeds and Confessions of Faith in Christendom and Beyond*, p. 142.

ance. It emphasizes the points of agreement before it affirms points of conscientious difference. To many Romanists it was an amazing revelation of the essential Catholicism of Lutheran teaching."[24] For some, like John Foxe, it was too tepid. He would later describe its propositions as intended for "weaklings newly weaned from their mother's milk of Rome."[25]

Even after the deaths of Henry and Thomas More, Cranmer moved slowly. His over-arching purpose was to create something which would have comparable status in the emerging Protestant world as that enjoyed by the Augsburg Confession. Cranmer was carefully balancing two goals that often do not mix well, doctrinal clarity and Christian unity.

Cranmer and the other Protestant reformers were carefully watching the on-again, off-again Council of Trent, convened in 1545 (not to end until 1563), which had been called within the Roman Church to deal with the theological and ecclesiastical issues created by (revealed by?) the Protestant Reformation. Cranmer did not want to make a definitive statement of what the Church of England believed which could subvert his other goal of getting a generally agreed statement that would provide a real alternative to the statements of Trent.

Quoting Thomas Rogers:

Cranmer had 'employed a great part of his time and study for the effecting of . . . a joint and common consent of all the churches . . . containing and expressing the sum and substance of that religion, which they do all both concordably teach and uniformly maintain' . . . 'every kingdom and free state, or principality' which had abandoned the Roman obedience 'should divulge a brief on that religion, which among themselves was taught and believed', and in England, that work was principally Cranmer's.[26]

---

24 Packer, *The Thirty-nine Articles*, p. 149.

25 Thomas, p. xxxvii.

26 MacCulloch, p. 503.

The effort to mold a comfortable yet comprehensive and co-gent doctrinal statement was at the heart of what the Protestant Reformation had been all about. Cranmer knew full-well that bishops and kings come and go, but he wanted the newly re-formed Church of England to rest on a more solid foundation than the shoulders of humankind. He wanted its roots deep in the Truth of the Gospel. The mechanism for that rootedness was a statement of faith to which all could look for guidance and to which all in authority must subscribe.

The Passion for Liturgy

Cranmer reasoned that theology ought to be imbedded in the liturgy so that it would be more easily imbibed by the people. But it was never Cranmer's intent to let the liturgy carry the theo-logical load. It is a bit disingenuous to criticize our brothers and sisters in the faith who claim that they have "no creed but the Bible" when some Anglicans have tried to say, in effect, "we have no creed but the liturgy." The Articles were a necessary ingredi-ent to the Reformation which Cranmer and others worked so diligently to effect.

As hard as it was, and still is, to change liturgical expression, it is the surest route to changing theological conviction. Cranmer knew that he could use the liturgical and worshiping life of the people to infuse them with the theology of the Reformation. "The 1549 book [of Common Prayer] gave witness to a characteristic Cranmerian principle: one should make haste slowly, and be sensitive to the prejudices of those Christians who had not yet been made conscious of their elect status, but one should never abandon the goal of reform."[27]

"The idea that the essence of Anglicanism is the Prayer Book, without the Articles, is a new idea, not rooted in the facts of his-tory at all, but developed in recent years in order that the group of churches which sends its bishops to Lambeth might with a good conscience call itself a Communion. . . ."[28]

---

27 MacCulloch, p. 411.

28 Packer, *The Thirty-nine Articles, Their Place and Use Today*, p. 5.

This, by the way, helps to answer the question of why the 1928 Prayer Book has been banned in all but a few places. It is being proscribed not because it is heretical (for it is not — if anything it is more orthodox than the book that replaced it), nor is it because of its anachronistic English (that same "problem" was easily "corrected" in the new hymnal, for example). It is anathematized because, when liturgy replaces verity as the highest value, liturgical conformity must necessarily take the place of doctrinal conformity. Thus are Anglicans bound not by the ties that bind, nor by the constraints of theological conviction, but we are bound by the binding of a book.

The Push for Confessional Articles

"The history of the Thirty-nine Articles effectively begins with several statements of faith published during the reign of Henry VIII, following the break with Rome in 1534. They were the Ten Articles of 1536, the *Institution of a Christian Man* of 1537 (also known as the 'Bishops' Book'), an unpublished set of 13 articles in 1538 done in cooperation with German Lutherans (with whom Cranmer was trying to forge a religious/political alliance), and *A Necessary Doctrine and Erudition for any Christian Man* of 1543 (also known as the 'King's Book')."[29]

The process may have proceeded in fits and starts but its goal was clear: to produce a comprehensive set of articles that would explicate the theology implicit in the liturgy, canons, and structures of the nascent church. In fact, Cranmer resisted efforts of moderates like Bishop Gardiner who felt that simply severing jurisdictional ties with the Pope was enough to reform the church. Cranmer wanted more than just a legal separation that would give the English Church some space. He wanted a theological foundation that was secure and could be turned to as a source of strength and guidance in the years ahead. His official title for the Ten Articles of 1536 spoke to this point: "Articles to establish Christian Quietness and Unity among Us and to avoid Contentious Opinions."

---

29   Miller, V. C., *The Lambeth Articles*, p. 5.

Elizabeth I
1533 — 1603

By 1549 Cranmer was calling for subscription to doctrinal articles for all new preachers and theological teachers.[30] Even though the new Prayer Book was in place, Cranmer was at work behind the scenes, trying to get his articles accepted by the bishops. Discussions continued into 1550, but he could not muster enough votes among bishops to get these new, Protestant articulations through. The Articles Cranmer presented to the bishops in 1551 were not publicized otherwise, and their status remained ambiguous. A year later, in 1552, the Privy Council sent a request to Cranmer asking for a copy of the Articles and enquired whether they had been issued "by any public authority or no."[31]

Cranmer continued to refine his Articles during the balance of the reign of Edward VI and even into the early stages of the reign of Mary. The major work of reform was put on hold, however, during Mary's bloody reign. It was during this time (in 1556) that Cranmer and others of like mind paid with their lives for their desire to return the Church of England to its Biblical roots.

When Mary died in 1558, the whole religious scene in England was very unsettled. The clergy were worried, the people were panicked, the world was watching. England had just experienced only its second woman monarch (the short and contentious reign of Matilda in the 12th century barely rates a footnote in history.)[32] Mary's brief but bloody reign had confirmed their worst fears about women sovereigns. Onto this rickety stage stepped one of the most towering figures in world history, Elizabeth.

She both wooed and wowed the people of England with her wisdom and her strength. She made peace abroad and peace at home. She settled England in the "new world" and

---

30   MacCulloch, p. 503.

31   Ibid., p. 504.

32   As a footnote to this footnote, mention should be made of the nine-day "reign" of Lady Jane Grey who, at age 16, was placed on the throne through the machinations of her father-in-law, John Dudley, Duke of Northumberland. This attempt to redirect the line of succession away from Roman Catholic rule under Mary Tudor failed. Lady Jane (Queen Jane?) was executed for treason on February 12, 1554, a martyr in the effort to bring the Protestant Faith and statesmanship to England.

she settled the church in the old world. While her personal piety was appropriately ambiguous for a political figure, she was wise enough to see that being the monarch of a Protestant country had advantages in terms of national sovereignty and identity. As supreme "governor" of the national church (she eschewed the title "head" which Henry had coveted) and as the Queen of the secular state, Elizabeth consolidated control of her various constituencies.

A key element in solidifying the nature of her rule was the establishment of clear guidelines in those areas of life deemed essential for national peace and stability. The religious life of the people was certainly one of these areas. There was no such thing as a "secular" state in the world at that time. Most leaders felt that religious conformity was as critical to national defense as good muskets. Social security depended as much on naves full of committed and obedient sinners as it did on navies full of committed and obedient sailors.

To that end, Elizabeth saw to it that the work so well begun by Cranmer and Ridley was brought to completion by Bps. Parker and Jewel. Once again, neither the crown nor the clergy were content to let liturgy alone carry the load of theology. Their work in refining and expanding the Articles issued forth in a preliminary set of Articles in 1563.

Thus, it was not until 15 years after Cranmer's death that the true value of the Articles was embraced by the English Church. In 1571, the final set of Articles was officially adopted under Queen Elizabeth I. They have been the official statement of Anglican Christianity ever since.

In 1628, the Royal Declaration of Charles I stated that "The Articles do contain the true doctrine of the Church of England, agreeable to God's word, which we do therefore ratify and confirm, requiring all our loving subjects to continue in the uniform profession thereof, and prohibiting the least difference from the said Articles." Further, they were to be understood in their "plain and full meaning" as found in their "literal and grammatical sense."

In 1721, the Crown issued a letter stating that the Articles were to be used as a test of true religion. In 1865, Queen Victoria dispensed with the requirement that new clergy perform Morning and Evening Prayer on their first Sunday but kept the requirement that all must publically read and assent to the Articles.

The essential status of the Articles in America during this period was equally clear.

Discussion Questions

1) John Wesley once said that hymns should be music for people who are not musicians and theology for people who are not theologians. To what extent does a person have to be a "theologian" to be a Christian?

2) Do you agree with Newman's quotation at the beginning of this chapter? Why or why not?

3) What are the implications of the fact that the New Testament is virtually silent on the issue of church government?

4) How important is theological and doctrinal clarity to you relative to the other reasons for joining a certain church? In reality, how does it compare with such issues as worship, music, location, friendly and sincere people, children's programs, etc?

5) Do people in the western world still care about theology? Explain your answer.

ઉ T·H·R·E·E ૭

A "New World"
But Not a New Theology

The Church of England was the greatest casualty of the American Revolution, being stripped almost overnight of its privileges, prestige, and support. As the church of royal officials it was disliked and distrusted.

Winthrop Hudson

J ust as the 16th century was a time of transition and turmoil, so also was the end of the 18th and the beginning of the 19th century a turbulent era for American Anglicans. A study of the conditions in the church at the beginning of the 19th millennium after Christ can do a lot to help faithful people prepare for the advent of the 21st century.

In 1801, Thomas Jefferson was inaugurated the third President of the United States. Before the Revolution, "Anglican clergy in the middle and northern colonies sought to impress the local populace by convening their conventions in the presence of the governor and having them preceded by a public procession of the clergy in gowns and cassocks."[33] After the Revolution, from the perspective of American Anglicans, one of their most cherished theological assumptions, the time-honored tradition of a strong connection between church and state, was formally severed.

Yet, for at least a season, American Anglicans could take some comfort in the fact that a very high percentage of the leaders of their country were Anglicans. Then, in short order, the highest

---

33 Hudson, Winthrop, *Religion in America*, p. 89.

office in the land went from being occupied by a deist Anglican (George Washington), to a deist Presbyterian who loathed Calvinism (John Adams)[34], to a deist/agnostic (Thomas Jefferson). Washington had made a show of his allegiance to the Anglican Church and its God. Adams was no sectarian, but he did authorize national days of fasting and prayer. Jefferson refused even to do that. Thus, by the year Jefferson took office, a trend was clearly emerging, and the trend was not a friendly one for the traditional alliance between church and state that Anglicans had not only come to expect, but which had been a basis for the foundation of their communion in the first place.

Anglicans in America were facing an unprecedented situation. For the first time, church and state would be separate. One wag has said that Anglicans could never decide if Bibles authorized kings or if kings authorized Bibles. American Anglicans faced a situation where kings and Bibles had no formal diplomatic relations at all. The chess game had changed. The bishop no longer stood between his sovereigns and their knights, he was off the board and out of the game. The firebrand Cotton Mather spoke for many a smoldering resentment when he said, "Let all mankind know that we came into the wilderness because we would worship God without that Episcopacy, that Common Prayer, and those unwarranted ceremonies with which the 'land of our forefathers' sepulchers had been defiled."[36]

The church responded wisely and well. Just as prayers for the king were altered to fit the new context, so were the Articles. The inherent theology, with its biblical respect for secular authority, was retained. But, references in Article XXXVII to the sovereign's power over the church were modified to fit the new conditions. Thus, the very presence of the Articles in America affirmed that one may honor the theological and biblical prin-

---

34   John Adams wrote the following to Thomas Jefferson: *"The Love of God and his Creation; Delight, Joy, Tryumph, Exultation in my own existence . . . are my religion. Howl, Snarl, Bite, Ye Calvinistick! . . . Ye will say, I am no Christian: I say Ye are no Christians . . ."* quoted from Gaustad, *A Documentary History of Religion in America: To the Civil War,* p. 296.

35   Hudson, p. 116.

36   Hudson, p. 100, 101.

ciple while, at the same time, altering the specific application for a particular time and place. By definition, all "Christian" theology is "incarnational" in this respect.

The Constitution of the American Episcopal Church, adopted in 1789, declared that the Articles of Religion should be in use in the American Church once they had been adopted. Official adoption did not take place until 1801.[37]

The subject of the Articles had been brought up at the convention of 1786. The version of the Articles proposed for adoption at that time numbered only 20 articles. These proposed, slimmed-down articles were rejected by the delegates. Concerned that their initial "rejection" by the delegates might doom them to a legal limbo, the convention of 1789 incorporated them, in principle, into the Constitution of the American Protestant Episcopal Church. The question of whether the American Church would have articles had been settled, even if the final form of the Articles was still to be determined. The question came up again in 1792 but was again tabled because of disagreement over the form they should take.

There were three major camps. Bishop Seabury felt that "all necessary doctrine should be comprehended in the Liturgy" but still realized "the inconveniences likely to result from there being no authoritative rule in the form of public confession [of faith]."[38] Bishop Madison, on the other hand, opposed the principle of having confessional articles at all. Bishop White favored having articles but did not believe subscription was necessary. The other bishops (Clagett and Provoost) offered no opinion on record.

Bp. White's convictions carried the day. This was not surprising. Colonialism had been very good to William White (1748-1836). He was born wealthy and well-connected and had been ordained in the Church of England. Yet, when revolution

---

37 Massey Shepherd has an excellent summary of the early history of the Articles in America in his *Oxford American Prayer Book Commentary*.

38 Shepherd, Massey Hamilton, *The Oxford American Prayer Book Commentary*, p. 601.

Bishop William White
1748 — 1836

came, he sided with the American patriots and served as chaplain to the Continental Congress. His pamphlet, *The Case of the Episcopal Churches in the United States Considered*, was written in 1782, only a few years after the United States came into existence. In it, he argued that the churches in the various states which had previously been identified with the Church of England, openly reorganize themselves under the new name chosen in Maryland, the Protestant Episcopal Church in the United States of America (PECUSA). He and other priests and lay people decided to call a "general convention" of this new organization to be held in Philadelphia in 1785. It was, therefore, largely through the leadership and vision of William White that the Anglican Church continued to exist in America at all.

While the delegates continued to haggle for several years over exactly what form these articles would take, two things were clear from the beginning: first, the American branch of the Anglican Communion would have a set of written articles of faith, and, second, that subscription would not be required because the Articles would be included in the Constitution of the Church. Thus, assent would be assumed and subsumed under the vow to uphold the doctrine and discipline of the church.

When Bishop Seabury died in 1796, his passing seemed to embolden the Connecticut delegation for they led the charge to get the Articles adopted in 1801, which they were. The only modifications to those articles current in England at the time were the necessary changes to the "political parts."

As the journal of the 1804 convention recorded: "A proposed Canon, concerning subscription to the Articles of the Church, was negatived, under the impression that a sufficient subscription to the Articles is already required in the 7th Article of the Constitution."[39]

Note again, subscription to the Articles was not required because they were already included in the Constitution of the Church adopted in 1789. It was believed by those present that when an ordinand vowed to uphold the doctrine and discipline of the Church, this included the Constitution which included

---

39 Hatchett, Marion, *Commentary on the American Prayer Book*, p. 588.

the Articles. This is why it is so pernicious that the Articles were removed from the Constitution of the American Church on the grounds that they were in the Prayer Book. They were in the Prayer Book because they were in the Constitution. Now, even though they remain the official doctrine of the Episcopal Church, they are in danger of being removed completely from the conscious life and the educated conscience of the church.

It is this tack that Massey Shepherd took when he wrote, "Inasmuch as the Articles are but one part of the Prayer Book, it is important to remember that the doctrine of the Anglican communion is enshrined in the Prayer Book as a whole. The Articles should be interpreted in the light of the teaching of the entire Prayer Book. They are not a norm by which the rest of the Prayer Book must of necessity be judged and explained."[40]

With all due respect, such a statement begs the question: What, then, is the standard by which items are included or excluded from the liturgical life of the church? Is doctrine explicit or implicit in the Prayer Book? Does not their "establishment" by special act of the General Convention in 1801 give the Articles some sort of an independent standing? Are the Articles, then, no different than the rubrics, or the prayer *For the Good Use of Leisure* (BCP p. 825), or the *Daily Devotions for Individuals and Families* (BCP p. 137)? Is this where we want to be as a church?

By the beginning of the 20th century, the presence of the Articles in the life of the Episcopal Church had become, for some, a matter of controversy and/or embarrassment. From 1907 until 1928, formal efforts were mounted to legally remove the Articles from the Constitution of the Episcopal Church. These moves failed. The Episcopal Church valued the Articles and wanted them to be a valued part of the continuing life of the Church, not just as an historic document.

The Lambeth Conference of Bishops in 1968 included an attempt to deal with the status of the Articles in the church. The Bishops "voted strongly for the proposal that each Province" consider three things: first, whether the Articles needed

---

40   Shepherd, *The Oxford American Prayer Book Commentary*, p. 601.

to be bound up with the Prayer Book, second, whether ordinands should still be required to assent to the Articles, and, third, how to ensure that any subscription which was required only be given in the context of the full range of the "inheritance of faith and within their historical context." Lambeth declarations do not have the force of law, but they do act as a barometer of the church's sentiments, at least at the higher altitudes.

Unfortunately, specific reference to the Articles was removed from the Constitution of the Episcopal Church at the 1988 General Convention.

Some would argue that it was meet and right so to do. After all, the General Convention guides the church through the contents of Canon Law and the *BCP*. But, the Articles are a special case — by design — and they just won't seem to go away.

The Book of Common Prayer introduces the Articles with the phrase: "As established by the Bishops, the Clergy, and the Laity of the Protestant Episcopal Church in the United States of America, in Convention, on the twelfth day of September, in the year of our Lord, 1801." The Articles had been included in the church's Constitution from the beginning in 1789.

It is significant that they were originally placed between the Psalter and the Ordinal. In that position they served as both a preface to the Ordinal and as a bridge between the liturgical prayers and praise of God's people and the convictions that undergirded those expressions of faith. The Articles were moved to the end of the book in 1886, where they remained until the 1979 book whence they were relegated to that newly created "Attic of Anglican Antiquities" known as the "Historical Documents" section.

What is an "historical document"? No one seems to know. Are they still binding on the conscience and conscious life of the church? Do we hold onto them? If so, how? Do we hold them aloft as an ideal? Do we hold them near, like a plumb line? Do we hold them in tension with our current theological convictions? Do we hold them in our hearts as sentimental keepsakes, reminders of a bygone era, only to be found in the rare documents section of Anglican theological schools? Are we moving toward the day when only canon lawyers and church historians will know what we believe?

"Excellent question, young man. You should be able to find a copy of the Articles in the rare book room of any competent theological library — Anglican of course. Good hunting and I hope you're not allergic to dust . . ."

In the minds of those who acted in 1801, "establishment" was a separate step from inclusion in the Constitution. It is curious, then, to read in White and Dykman's analysis that the Articles were "'established'" by their inclusion in Article X.[41] If "establishment" had been synonymous with inclusion in the Constitution, the church would not have "established" them again in 1801.

There was a conscious, continuing effort to strengthen their position within the early Episcopal Church. Not only were they included as part of the original Constitution in 1789 *and* formally "established" at the General Convention in 1801; they were protected by a special action of the General Convention in 1829 when the church guarded against "hasty alterations" by including them in the clause of the Constitution that made alteration a matter of due process. Thus, in the early years of the American Church's life, a clear pattern of honoring and protecting the Articles can be discerned.

It is also important to note that the rationale given in 1985/88 was neither theological nor even pastoral, but merely procedural. It was a "simplification," done to "delete those matters that are repetitious of other contents of *The Book of Common Prayer*."[42] First, we may ask where else in the *BCP* is the content of the Articles duplicated? Second, it is important to note that the stated rationale is very different from the one given when the matter was first proposed.

In 1907, the committee report that recommended deletion of the Articles argued that their presence in *The Book of Common Prayer*:

> tends to demoralization of both Clergy and the Laity, of the Clergy since it leaves them helpless to answer with any defi-

41   White, Edwin and Jackson Dykman, *Annotated Constitution and Canons*, p. 136.

42   *The Blue Book*, 1988, p. 13.

niteness the question, what is the Doctrine of the Episcopal Church? of the Laity because they are thoroughly perplexed by the sight of what looks to be a Creed supplementary to the other Creeds, while at the same time they are assured by their spiritual guides that it is something about which they need not at all concern themselves. Why should it be here in the Prayer Book, they ask, if it be unimportant? Why, if it be important, should we be told as Laymen we need not care?[43]

To the extent that this rather guileless paragraph spoke for the leadership of the church in the early part of this century, it is not hard to see why the Articles were a stumbling block. In their 1982 commentary, after quoting the almost eight-decades old paragraph above, White and Dykman wondered at their continued inclusion in Article X. One may ask, why not wonder at the "spiritual guides" who guided their followers away from the solid food of theology and who implied that a knowledge of one's theological heritage is "unimportant"? And how would removal of the Articles help these "helpless" "spiritual guides" to answer with "definiteness" about the Doctrine of the Episcopal Church?

Alarmingly, it appears that less than 200 years after the Articles were consciously and rigorously included in the life of the American Church, repeatedly confirmed and established by numerous acts of the General Convention of the American Church, received, honored and consistently applied to countless controversies within the American Church, the Articles now find themselves to have become at best *adiaphora*, and at worst a scandal.[44]

Have the Articles been proven to be false and misleading? No. Is the content of the Articles replicated elsewhere in the life

---

43 White and Dykman, p. 136.

44 In 1981, Steven Applegate produced an intriguing article, "The Rise and Fall of the Thirty-Nine Articles: An Inquiry into the Identity of the Protestant Episcopal Church in the United States." The article chronicles the efforts of William Reed Huntington, author of *Tract XCI*, to have the *Articles of Religion* removed from *The Book of Common Prayer* and placed in an "Archive of English Religion." The author is content to simply raise questions, and he leans toward a too-tidy conspiracy theory. But the questions it raises are important ones. And, if not a conspiracy, the facts as they developed make William Reed Huntington something of a prophet. *Historical Magazine of the Protestant Episcopal Church, 50:409-421*, December, 1981.

of the American Church? No. Why then is there this almost con-
spiratorial campaign to slowly and slyly remove them to the
darkest corners of the church?

Discussion Questions

1)   With new churches and denominations springing up
      every day, do you think it is important to be part of a
      church that has a rich history? Why or why not?

2)   Do you think there has been a determined, if vaguely
      subconscious, effort to remove the Articles from the life of
      the American Church? Why or why not?

3)   Have you ever heard a sermon or a teaching on the Ar-
      ticles in any church you have ever attended? If so, what
      affect did it have on you?

4)   How has the "level playing field" and the "open market"
      of American religious life made Christianity more vital
      and viable?

5)   Is society going too far in trying to remove religion from
      the public square? What might be some differences be-
      tween "freedom of religion" and "freedom from religion"?

☙ F · O · U · R ❧

A Most Viable *Via Media!?*

[We dare not] declare the Church a kind of Noah's Ark, within which every kind of opinion and creed shall dwell safe and undisturbed, and the only terms of communion shall be the willingness to come inside and leave your neighbor alone.

Bishop J. C. Ryle

I have on my shelf a book sub-titled *Neither Catholic nor Protestant* by Walter Klaassen. The book was written to show a third way, a middle ground, a *via media* between the Roman Church and the Protestant Church. But, it's not about Anglicans. The book was written by and about Anabaptists. Does the middle of the road belong to whomever gets there first or is there an historical and theological consensus that can be applied to aid in our discernment? We believe there is ample historical precedent to declare Anglicanism to be a true *via media*. But a *via* between what other *media*?

Philosophy may move between thesis, anti-thesis toward synthesis, but there is no such thing as *theos*, *anti-theos* moving toward *syn-theos*. As one wise theologian once remarked, "If someone says 'Jesus is Lord,' and someone else says 'Jesus is not Lord,' the answer is NOT that 'Jesus is Lord some of the time.'" God is God, and His Son claimed to be "the Truth" (*John 14:6*). Ergo, theologians are not free to compromise His Truth. Unless a *via media* can claim that it aligns with the Truth, its good intentions only pave the way to . . . well . . .

While, in the minds of some, "Cranmer's *First Prayer Book* was a brilliant piece of studied ambiguity,"[45] it was not Cranmer's

---

45 Spitz, Lewis, *The Renaissance and Reformation Movements*, Vol. II, p. 460.

passionate commitment to "ambiguity" that earned him a martyr's death. The existential disciplines of prayer and worship are rooted in, not coincidental with, the propositional discipline of theology. Cranmer knew the difference. When we make all theology *adiaphora*, we ourselves are perilously close to another kind of flames. "As their title declares, the Articles were drawn up 'for the avoiding of diversities of opinions, and for the establishing of consent touching true religion,' a purpose which deliberate ambiguity would actually have defeated."[46]

Properly understood, the Anglican *via media* was not then, and is not now, the path of least resistance. "Anglican moderation is the policy of reserving strong statement and conviction for the few things that really deserve them."[47] The growing catechetical movement within our church is a testimony to our people's hunger for substance to undergird their experience.

Anglican comprehensiveness was never intended to sacrifice the "Anglicanism" for the "comprehensiveness." The two terms are not interchangeable. Comprehensiveness is modified grammatically and moderated theologically by its marriage to historic Anglicanism. And those whom God has joined together, let man not unknot. Without that safeguard, the Anglican Church is in danger of becoming a kind of "league of religions," to use Dr. Adam Vidler's colorful phrase.

Being the shortest of all the Reformation confessions, the Articles are already fairly minimal, which combined with their widespread neglect over the years, has led to the curious and entertaining invocation of a heathen god into the mix. Note how these comrades in the faith (who likely actually agree with each other on most points) invoke the demi-god as a sort of *deus ex machina* . . .

- *From its beginning as a distinct category of Christianity, Anglicanism has shown two different faces. It has from the time of the English Reformation been a Janus.*
  Paul Zahl

---

46   Packer, *Thirty-nine Articles*, p. 35.

47   O'Donovan, Oliver, *On the Thirty-nine Articles: A Conversation with Tudor Christianity*, p. 14.

- *Neglecting the Articles creates a problem of Anglican integrity . . . On this question, as on others, the Church of England causes real scandal by appearing, Janus-like, to face both ways.* J. I. Packer

- *In this homily ['Of ceremonies: why some should be abolished and some retained'], Cranmer spoke Janus- like both to those who were 'addicted to their old customs' and to those who were 'so new fangle [sic] that they would innovate all thing, and so do despise the old that nothing can like them, but that is new.'* Diarmaid MacCulloch

Janus was the Roman god of beginnings (hence "January"). He was also the god of endings. Sort of like the ambiguous but buoyant salutation "aloha" which means both "hello" and "goodbye." He was, literally, a two-faced deity who stood guard in his temple with doors open to the east — to greet the rising sun — and to the west — to preside over its setting. Is it significant that Janus was the Roman god of morning prayer?

One may legitimately ask whether, by embracing this vision of ourselves, we have opened the door to a type of ambiguity that flows neither hot nor cold. Being referred to as "two-faced" is not often a compliment, especially when we claim to represent a God who describes His blessing in terms of turning His face towards His people: *"Tell Aaron and his sons, 'This is how you are to bless the Israelites. Say to them:*

"'"The Lord bless you and keep you; the Lord make his face shine upon you and be gracious to you; the Lord turn his face toward you and give you peace"'" (*Numbers 6:23-26*).

Perhaps it is also significant that the doors to the temple of Janus were only kept open during war. The Romans wanted to make certain that their enemies, and their own people, knew that no matter who started the war, Rome would finish it. In that sense, the image of Janus affirms the truth that beginnings and endings are not unrelated. To lose track of the beginning is to make the end uncertain. That is the danger we face today.

The Articles have guided the Anglican Church through at least three major attempts to compromise its unique identity and to loose it from its beginnings: Puritanism, Romanism, and

Anabaptism. Ironically, or providentially, these three forces are also present today in Anglicanism — perhaps it will always be so — and the Articles can provide a clear and consistent response to these challenges to the traditional Anglican understanding of The Faith.

Puritanism

In 1595, in reaction against Hooker's *Laws of Ecclesiastical Polity*, some Puritan-minded churchmen met at Lambeth to respond to the issues raised by an ardent but anonymous tract (*A Christian Letter* on Hooker's *Laws of Ecclesiastical Polity*) and by a series of contentious sermons given by members of the Cambridge community. The group produced a document called "The Lambeth Articles." These were intended to supplement the then 20 year-old *Thirty-nine Articles* in order to "correct" a perceived softness and/or vagueness pertaining to the doctrines of election, reprobation, and justification.

The sermons that provoked the gathering at Lambeth were delivered by William Barrett and William Whitaker. Barrett, from Caius College, Cambridge, argued against the "assurance of salvation" he perceived to be inherent in the Articles. He also attacked Calvin, Beza and other Reformation theologians. Barrett, in turn, was responding to a sermon preached earlier that year by William Whitaker, Master of St. John's College, Cambridge and Regius Professor of Divinity. Whitaker's sermon warned of what he perceived as creeping Pelagianism on the campus of Cambridge. Even though Whitaker was a moderate, non-presbyterian Puritan, his views provided a handy jumping off point for Barrett.

Barrett was ordered to retract his teachings, which he did reluctantly. Copies of Barrett's reluctant retraction were given to Archbishop Whitgift. He passed them on to his chaplains (Lancelot Andrewes and Adrian Savaria). Whitgift modified the original articles drafted by Whitaker to make them appeal to a broader constituency, though they still pushed the Calvinist agenda. When Queen Elizabeth found out about them, she stopped their distribution. Ultimately they were rejected.

The Calvinist and Puritan agendas continued in England for several more decades. English Calvinism would continue to press forward, through the Hampton Court Conference and the Synod of Dort, to the Westminster Assembly where the Westminster Confession and Catechism were created and the English Presbyterian movement took shape. But, the seminal point of this episode was that the Anglican Church had been given a golden opportunity to turn toward a more radical Protestantism and had turned it down. The Articles remained intact and the inherent moderation of Anglicanism was affirmed. "The point is that this set of 'Calvinist' beliefs, assumed by Whitgift and Whitaker to be the consensus, did not win outright."[48]

In its extreme forms, Puritanism can represent an overly-scrupulous, law-centered focus to the Christian life. While the early Puritans were devoted to the Bible as their guide, some of their descendants have, in a sincere attempt to be obedient to the Bible, gone beyond the Bible in codifying conduct. Christians must be ever mindful of Paul's admonition to the Christians at Corinth: *"Do not go beyond what is written. Then you will not take pride in one man over against another"* (I Corinthians 4:6). This unhealthy form of Puritanism is present today in the forms of certain tendencies toward cultural fundamentalism and the assertion that the Bible is not just the primary guide but the only guide for life.

First, cultural fundamentalism is the belief that Christians are those who, in the words of the ancient rhyme, "Don't smoke, dance or chew or go with girls who do." It manifests itself in the honest and faithful efforts of Christian people to be obedient to the commands of Christ. The unfortunate result, however, is all too often a neo-pharisee-ism that strains out gnats but swallows camels.

Second, while we certainly want to affirm the Scriptures as the only sure and certain guide for human conduct and that no action of the church may contradict God's Word Written (see Articles VI & XX), it is naive and disingenuous to affirm that the answers to all of life's quandaries are found explicitly in the text

---

48 Miller, V. C., p. 91.

of the Bible. That is why the Anglican Church's informal, but no less real, dogma of using Scripture, Tradition, and Reason is so helpful in addressing life's distresses. *Sola Scriptura (Scripture Alone)* makes a lovely and riveting motto, but nobody lives like that, really.

Romanism

A more famous, and many would say more successful, challenge to the Articles came in the form of the famous *Tract XC* (*Tract 90*), written by John Henry Newman and published in 1841. At that time, Newman was an Episcopal priest. He would later become a Roman Catholic Cardinal.

Newman left the Anglican Church in 1845 to pursue holy orders in the Roman Church. Everybody loves a convert — to their side — and he became quite a celebrity. His wisdom and eloquence won many converts to his position and, for a generation, he effectively silenced Anglican Protestant apologists.

Then, in December, 1863, a Protestant polemicist, the Rev. Charles Kingsley, intensified an attack he had previously launched against John Newman for his decision to leave the Anglican Church and embrace the Church of Rome. This gave Newman the opportunity for which he had waited almost 20 years. Like Augustine before him, Newman sought to show his convictions through the medium of autobiographical narrative. Newman wrote: "As I have already said, there are but two alternatives, the way to Rome, and the way to Atheism: Anglicanism is the halfway house on the one side, and Liberalism is the halfway house on the other."[49]

If Newman is right that Anglicanism is merely a "halfway house" then this house is no home. If all roads lead to Rome, including the *via media*, then the Anglican Church has no independent validity except as a compromise between "Atheism" and "Rome." The point of Newman's attack on Anglican validity was the Articles. In order to demonstrate their amenability to Roman

---

49 Newman, John Henry, *History of My Religious Opinions*, p. 204.

Catholic interpretation, Newman had to make a clear break with the obvious intent of those who drafted the Articles in the 16th century. He wrote: "It is a duty which we owe both the Catholic Church and to our own, to take our reformed confessions in the most Catholic sense they will admit; we have no duties toward the framers."[50]

He went on to say that "The Protestant Confession was drawn up with the purpose of including Catholics; and Catholics now will not be excluded. What was an economy of the reformers, is a protection to us. What would have been a perplexity to us then, is a perplexity to Protestants now. We could not then have found fault with their words; they cannot now repudiate our meaning."[51]

Even the most ardent Reformed Protestant had to admit that his critique was brilliant right from the start. For example, in his discussion of Article VI (about the Scriptures and the statement that those "of whose authority was never any doubt in the Church") he points out that there was quite considerable doubt about some of the books (he mentions Hebrews and Revelation) in certain parts of the church. Therefore, what is meant by "the Church" must not mean individual congregations or even dioceses, or provinces. The Church must be The Church Catholic, gathered together for the purpose of forming an opinion about the issue at hand. This, of course, did not happen until over a hundred years had elapsed since the death of Christ. Therefore, he reasoned from the text of the article, The Church to which it refers is the Roman Church. But it was in those articles which most directly attacked the Medieval Roman Church that Newman made the most creative discourse.

When I retrieved a copy of *Tract XC* from the shelves of the seminary library, it fell open to Newman's comments on Article XXII, the one about purgatory. An examination of the binding showed that this old volume had been repeatedly opened to that spot, and few others. This is not surprising for it is here that Newman made his most careful and colorful distinction. "Not

---

50 Newman, John Henry, *Tract XC*, p. 129.

51 Ibid., p. 134.

every doctrine on these matters is a fond thing, but the *Romish* doctrine."[52]

The biggest problem *Tract XC* raised was not that the Articles were "patient of Catholic interpretation," but that what they taught was not nearly as taut as they thought. It must be said, however, that if a document fails because it is capable of widely variant interpretations, the American Constitution and even the Scriptures themselves fail the test.

Newman's critique of the Articles fit the temper of his times. The "Oxford Movement" was gaining steam and there was a move toward the majesty and solidarity of Rome in the middle to the late 19th century. Several other commentaries on the Articles appeared during this period including one by Bishop A.P. Forbes, *An Explanation of the Thirty-nine Articles*, published in 1867.

Did Newman's hermeneutic[53] doom the Articles to a Valhalla of vagueness, or did he show once and for all that the Articles really say nothing different than the Roman Church has said all along? Not really.

First, as to Newman's hermeneutic, "It would be incorrect to say that Newman had abandoned the historical principle altogether. A fairer statement would be that he was applying the same principle to the answering of a new question, namely how much common ground the Articles retained with Roman Catholicism, instead of the customary one, how far they dissociated the Church of England from it."[54] In the wake of the Oxford movement, Newman was trying to answer a new question using an old text. He succeeded in showing that, if the framers' original intent is ignored (and that is a huge IF), combined with some clever and creative plumbing, the Articles can be interpreted in such a way that they do not totally discard Roman tendencies. Historically speaking, this is not a great insight. As we have discussed above, the Articles were intended to put forth a moder-

---

52 Newman, *Tract XC*, p. 139.

53 *Hermeneutics* is the art/science of interpreting scripture. A person's hermeneutic will often determine how a particular passage is interpreted and/or applied.

54 Packer, *The Thirty-nine Articles*, p. 39.

ate and concilliatory Protestantism, not a bridge-burning, rock-throwing Protestantism. They succeeded. But, their place in the middle of the *via media* is not altered.

The Articles are highly adaptable, within limits. Their presence in America and around the world attests to that. Yet, the Protestant Episcopal Church is a Protestant Church. A recent challenge to separately incorporate the name "Protestant Episcopal Church in the United States of America"(PECUSA) as opposed to the name "Episcopal Church in the United States of America" (ECUSA) showed that the word and the concept of being "Protestant" is still something that the Episcopal Church wants to hold onto. Just as the mid-point of the continental United States is still well east of the continental divide, so also is the *via media* still well into Protestant territory. If anything, recent actions by the General Convention of ECUSA (the mandatory ordination of women, for example) have made any future reunion with Rome even more unlikely.

Newman's critique raises another question: Are either of these terms either redundant or oxymoronic?

- Anglo-Catholic

- Protestant Episcopal

If Newman had his way, the term "Anglo-Catholic" would be redundant because any good Anglican would, by definition, be a good Catholic. On the other hand, the term "Protestant Episcopal" would be oxymoronic because one cannot have it both ways. Flip the views 180° and you have the formula advocated by more Protestant Anglicans.[55] Any objective view of the recent history of Anglicanism will show that this face of the Anglican "Janus" has been sorely neglected in recent decades. It is time to once again reaffirm that this is a "Protestant" Church with all the richness and splendor and energy that entails.

Such an affirmation could not come at a better time because there is a move toward Rome within the Anglican Church today. Men and women of faith are looking for stability and his-

---

55 For an excellent summation of this viewpoint, see Paul Zahl's book *The Protestant Face of Anglicanism* published in 1997 by Eerdmans.

toric continuity. They are seeking authority and a magisterium that is willing to make a stand for "the faith once delivered to the saints." Is Rome (or Orthodoxy) the only place left for Christians who want not just a liturgy that honors historic continuity but also a theology that makes that same commitment?

No. The Articles clearly place Anglicanism within the historic framework of orthodox Christianity. Their statements of orthodoxy are unequivocal and their pedigree is impeccable.

Anabaptism

Even though the English Articles are consistently painted as the *via media* between the Roman Church and the then emerging Protestant Churches on the continent, the reality was that the Articles were rarely invoked against Romans or "mainline" Protestants such as Lutherans and/or Presbyterians. The leavening of the Articles was most often leveled against the Anabaptists. The label "Anabaptist" (literally "over-again baptizers") was used to cover a variety of fairly extreme non-conformists. Webster defines "Anabaptist" as "any member of a radical 16th-century sect of the Reformation originating in Switzerland, often persecuted because they opposed the taking of oaths, infant baptism, military service, and the holding of public office."

These Christian folk were the original "enthusiasts." They were:

- Anti-hierarchical in an age when hierarchy meant stability.

- Spirit-led in an age that valued conformity to visible authority.

- Anti-creedal in an age that valued propositional statements of belief and conviction.

- Anti-clerical in an age when the clergy were held in high esteem and which saw, in the "parson" the "person" who held the town together.

We can also see shades of this exuberant non-conformity in some of the Charismatic expressions of Christianity today. Such antinomian antics can be refreshing and renewing. At the very least, Christian people who bring an understanding of The Faith which is radically different from our own force us to think.

On a more ominous note, we can also see some of the extremes to which this can lead as we reflect on the inroads which the New Age Movement has made into the Church. A fairly wholesale rejection of absolutes has accompanied this radical internalization of faith. It often presents itself wrapped in gentle-sounding language about being "open to new truths," being "spiritual," and as a way to respond to the baptismal vow to "seek and serve Christ in all persons."

Many of the Anabaptists believed the locus of truth and spirituality to be the inner self, unmediated by the Spirit of God and unregulated by His precepts. In this deceptive "theology," the objective word of God, the objectively and historically discerned truths of propositional revelation, the visible church and its ministrations, and all such "mundane" things are deemed either unnecessary or inferior. There is an incipient and subtle gnosticism[56] in this sort of spirituality.

A couple good rules of thumb: See especially Articles XXIII and XXXV regarding who should be qualified to teach, preach, and preside in the church. Be wary of those types of "spirituality" that require telephone calls to "900" numbers or insist that the seeker have a credit card handy when calling.

Also, honestly seek to determine under whose authority any given "church" and clergy exist and minister. To whom are they accountable?

---

56 One of the earliest heresies, gnosticism is the belief in a secret "knowledge" which alone can lead one to God.

Discussion Questions ————————————————

1)   Have you found it to be a comfort or not that Anglicanism often presents itself as a "Janus"?

2)   What are the good sides of Puritanism, Romanism, and Anabaptism? What do they offer the larger Church?

3)   Have you encountered tendencies toward Puritanism, Romanism, or Anabaptism in the Anglican Church?

4)   Why do you think it might be helpful to draw a careful distinction between cultural fundamentalism and Christian fundamentalism?

⚜ F · I · V · E ⚜

Are the Articles Anglican?

The Church of England, at the present time [1939], exhibits a doctrinal incoherence which has no parallel in any other church claiming to be traditionally orthodox. . . . The raison d'être of subscription to the Thirty-nine Articles is the necessity, in a divided Christendom, of agreeing on a version of the Catholic faith. In the Articles we have the Anglican version of the Catholic tradition of Faith and Discipline. It is not open to any loyal Anglican to form any other.

Herbert Hensley Henson, Bishop of Durham

As the 16th century came to a close, the Church of England was facing the perceived need to articulate its unique role in Christendom. To argue that the intent of the founders of the Anglican Community was to let the liturgy alone carry the doctrinal load is to ignore the fact that *The Book of Common Prayer* was settled in 1559, yet for two decades before that date and for 12 years after, the church struggled to define its faith through the use of articles. It finally did so in 1571 with the adoption of the *Thirty-nine Articles*.

In 1996 the Episcopal Church set about to try one of its bishops for breaking with the doctrine and discipline of the church. The trial never took place because the court held that no "core doctrine" had been violated. That phrase, "core doctrine," struck many a nerve and stuck in many a craw. Does the Episcopal Church have a doctrinal core apart from the ecumenical creeds of Christendom and/or the liturgy of the *BCP*? In an effort to answer that vexing question, many people have turned to 16th century Anglican divine, Richard Hooker.

Richard Hooker
1554 — 1600

It has become an almost *a priori* truth that "it is really unhistorical to speak of 'Anglicans' and 'Anglicanism' before 1593, the year that Richard Hooker published his great work *Of the Laws of Ecclesiastical Polity . . .* "[57] But, we agree with W. Taylor Stevenson that "if it can be said that anyone is the definitive Anglican theologian, then that person is Thomas Cranmer." It is not overly-simplistic to say that what Cranmer defined, Hooker refined. Hooker played Aristotle to Cranmer's Plato, the true genius of whose theological system lay in its ability to be refined.

What would Cranmer have said if confronted with the statement that "there is no distinctive Anglican theology?" The fact that he worked so hard to conceive, draft, revise, and establish "articles" articulating the unique convictions of Anglicanism speaks to the point. There is strong evidence that Cranmer was hard at work on a doctrinal statement as early as 1550, long before he was directed to do so by "the king and privy council." Their goal was"the preserving and maintaining of peace *and unity of doctrine* in this Church, that being finished they might be set forth by public authority."[58] In 1553, Cranmer presented his *Forty-two Articles* to his church and his crown. They were to be "the last of his major contributions to the development of Anglicanism."[59]

Let us look at Cranmer's work through Hooker's tri-focal lens: Scripture, Tradition, and Reason. Hooker's most incisive insight was that God's Truth is discerned through a threefold test. First, what does the Scripture teach? If Scripture is clear, that is the answer. If Scripture is silent or ambiguous, what has been the practice of the people of God at all times and in all places? In what has become known as the "Vincentian Canon, " St. Vincent of Lérins stated that the test of ecumenical orthodoxy was *quod ubique, quod semper, quod ab omnibus creditum est* ('what has been believed everywhere, always and by all').

---

57 Dugmore, C. W., "Foundation Documents of the Faith," p. 166.

58 Chadwick, Owen, *The Reformation*, p. 71 ff.

59 Noll, Mark, *Confessions and Catechisms of the Reformation*, p. 211.

If Tradition is silent or ambiguous, human Reason (in Hooker's thought more like common sense than rationalism) would settle the issue. This three-fold test of truth distinguished Anglicanism from more radical forms of Protestantism that advocated the use of Scripture alone (*Sola Scriptura*) to resolve theological or ecclesiastical disputes. Does the founding document of Anglicanism meet the requirements to be considered truly Anglican? Are the Articles Scriptural, Traditional, and Reasonable?

Are the Articles Scriptural?

The simple answer is, "Yes." Volumes have been written over centuries showing that the Articles accord with the teachings of Scripture. In a sense, that is why they were written in the first place. As J. I. Packer has rightly said, "What are creeds for? To hold the Church to the Bible." The Articles themselves set Scripture as the standard. (See Articles VI and XX in Chapter Seven of this book.) If anything, it is their strict adherence to Scripture that has made the Articles so controversial in the Anglican Church today. Granted, they betray a 16th century hermeneutic (the art/science of interpreting Scripture). That does not make them any less valuable or authoritative.

After the General Convention in 1925, a move was made to remove the Articles from the proposed "new" Prayer Book, the 1928 book. Writing to the point, Dr. William Morehouse said, "Everybody knows they [the Articles] are misleading and greatly misunderstood, and written in long involved sentences in a language four centuries ago, and that their teaching value today is almost nil."[60]

Yet, no one complains that 'being of one substance with the Father' (the *homoousion* of the Nicene Creed) is a foolish or obscure phrase, even though in our modern culture the word "substance" for most people does not have a metaphysical but only a chemical meaning.[61] We know how to put the debate about the

---

60   Grammar, Carl, "The Meaning of the Thirty-nine Articles."

61   Packer, *The Thirty-nine Articles*, p. 39.

Nicene Creed into context. We also rejoice and affirm its time-less import. The Nicene Creed betrays a fourth century hermeneutic but its antiquity and its clarity ensure that its value transcends the shifting sands of time and the whims of culture.

For more references for the various articles, see the commentary in Chapter Seven.

Are the Articles Traditional?

Again, the simple answer is "Yes." There is a sense in which they are "traditional" precisely because they are the Anglican Tradition. The Articles helped to create the Anglican Church. They had their genesis even before the Anglican Church came into being as a distinct theological/ecclesiastical entity in the 16th century. But their heritage is even more ancient than that.

The word "tradition" literally means to "hand something over." (Hence the word "traitor" from the same root). Our tradition is that which has been handed over to us. It is, therefore, our obligation to continue that process by faithfully handing it on to the next generation. Did the Articles faithfully reflect the Apostolic and Patristic heritage of the Church? Did the Articles faithfully pass on those verities to the following generations? Yes.

The Articles were not an attempt to create a new Faith. They were grounded in the conviction that the Medieval Church needed to be "*re*-formed," not created anew. The Medieval Church had departed from the beliefs and practices of the ancients. The Articles, like most of the other Protestant confessions of the 16th century, were an attempt to demonstrate that the Reformation was a return to the "purest ages of Christianity."

In the middle of the 19th century, doubts were raised about the antiquity of the theology contained in the Articles. In response, various scholars wrote volumes to show that the Articles had ancient authority, not only from Scripture, but also from the Church Fathers. In 1835, Oxford's Henry Cary wrote *Testimonies of the Fathers* to show how the Articles are supported by the teaching of the Church Fathers from the apostolic age to the 4th century. In it he wrote, "A principle which especially characterizes the Church of England, and distinguishes her from every other reformed communion, is her marked and avowed adherence to the Catholic faith as received in the primitive and purest ages of Christianity." In 1848, Richard Kidd wrote *Testimonies and Authorities, Divine and Human, in Confirmation of the Thirty- nine Articles of The Church of England* as another effort to show the ancient authority of the Articles. Most famous of all these efforts was John Newman's famous *Tract XC*. In this regard, at least, Newman's tract was a two-edged sword. By showing that the Articles were "patient of Catholic interpretation," he also demonstrated that they were equally patient in translating historic orthodoxy, whether it be Patristic, Medieval, or Scholastic.

Are the Articles Reasonable?

Yes, the Articles are reasonable *insofar as reason may discern*. In other words, there are things in the Articles that transcend human reason. That does mean they are *un*-reasonable. In that regard, what could be more unreasonable than the doctrine of the Incarnation? There is nothing common-sensical about God's *hesed* or *agape*[62] love as it is revealed in Scripture or on Calvary. As the Apostle Paul observed, there is a sense in which the Gospel is "foolishness" to those outside the covenant community. Anglican church historian Dr. Geoffrey Bromiley overstates the case only slightly when he says "the verities expressed in the Articles are the verities of the Gospel which must be the confession of any true church of Jesus Christ. Acceptance of the Articles is acceptance of the Gospel."[63]

But, having said that, the Articles are reasonable in precisely the sense I said we should not use the term "reason." They are rational. They proceed logically from their premises, which are the text of Holy Scripture and the ecumenical creeds of the Church.

Those articles that can be said to give the most offense to human reason, at least late 20th century human reason, have to

---

62 *Hesed* and *agape* are the Hebrew and Greek words, respectively, for God's "steadfast love" and God's "unconditional love."

63 Bromiley, Geoffrey, "Evangelism and the Anglican Articles 1563-1963," p. 590.

do with the mind of God as it is revealed in Scripture. Because they are rooted in exegesis (the art/science of interpreting scripture) and not reason, these articles are not amenable to either reasonable defense *or* reasonable attack. They make no claim to be reasonable. They are descriptive of the text of Scripture, not prescriptive of the way humankind wishes things to be.

"The Thirty-nine Articles do not claim to be a pleasant doctrine, or even doctrine which is easily commendable to reason. They do, however, very definitely claim that they are the consequences of statements of biblical truth, that is, that they are agreeable to the Word of God."[64]

One is reminded of C. S. Lewis' wise comment concerning those who wish that true religion were without affront or complication. "It is no good asking for a simple religion," said C. S. Lewis. "After all, real things are not simple. . . . as if 'religion' were something God invented, and not His statement to us of certain quite unalterable facts about His own nature."[65] In this most important sense, God Himself may seem "unreasonable" to our limited human intellects.

But what about Experience?

In recent years, some have sought to add a fourth "leg" to Hooker's "three-legged stool." The trouble with this, as anyone who has ever tried to build a table knows, three legs are inherently more stable than four. The proposed fourth leg is "experience."

It is easy to see why some would want to add it to the mix. First, everybody has experienced experience — it is the great common denominator of sentient life. Second, such an emphasis is congenial to the individualistic temperament of our times. Third, it is the contemporary trump card to any discussion on virtually anything: "Well, that hasn't been my experience" or its corollary "Well, that may be true for you

---

64   Knox, David Broughton, *The Thirty-nine Articles: The Historic Basis of the Anglican Faith*, p. 58.

65   Lewis, C. S., *Mere Christianity*, pp. 46, 47.

but it's not true for me" are guaranteed to either end any discussion or heat it until it boils over and ruins the evening.

Even though the Articles were composed in a day when
Hooker had not even attached the first three legs to his stool, let
alone this fashionable fourth, we must address this issue. If we
do not, it will appear we are ducking it.

Yes, God does meet us through our experiences. That is part
of God's plan. Experience is the journey, but theology is the map
that makes the journey meaningful. Scripture, Tradition, and
Reason give context to the experiences of life.

Think of Scripture, Tradition, and Reason as the three sides
of a doorway. Experience is the floor. The floor is everywhere
present. It is the ground on which we walk. It is always there.
But, without the three sides of the doorway, there would be no
way to identify when we have moved from one place to another.
When, in our walking about, we go through a doorway, delineated by its three sides, we know we have moved from one defined place to another. So it is with our theology.

Efforts to add experience to the defining characteristics of
Anglican theology beg the obvious. Experience is part of theological reflection, but only because it is part of everything. A
floor is present in a doorway, but the floor does not define the
door. Yet, it is on the floor that we travel through the doorway.
Experience is not denigrated by being put in its proper context.

Thus we see that the defining document of Anglicanism is,
in every sense of the word, Anglican. It accords with Scripture,
Tradition, and Reason. It can verify the experiences of God's
people by putting them into a theological context that is both
faithful to the Truth of the Gospel and uniquely congenial to
Anglican insights.

The Articles, indeed any confession of faith, cannot create an
encounter with the Living God. Confessions, like "witnesses,"
are, by definition, *ex post facto*. They cannot create an event or
an encounter, only testify to or help to clarify it. God is personal and, as such, must be encountered in a personal way. Theology is no substitute for a personal encounter with the living
Christ any more than studying a map is a substitute for taking a
journey. Jesus, the incarnate Lord and the living Christ, invites

us into a relationship with Himself through faith, not just to believe certain things about Him, even if they are all true.

But, without some way to (A) differentiate our encounters and (B) communicate our experiences, all religious discourse (even liturgy) becomes meaningless. Allow me to illustrate my point with a simple example — imagine this everyday exchange:

"When you get to Springfield, look up my friend Jim. His phone number is 123-4567. He is about six feet tall with dark hair and brown eyes and he loves Chinese food."

A week later: "Did you meet my friend Jim?'

"Yes. I called 987-6543 and met with a fellow who was about five feet tall, with blond hair and blue eyes. We ate at an Italian place because he said Chinese food doesn't agree with him."

"Well, it sounds like you had a good time, but the fellow you met was not my friend Jim."

"Who are you to critique my experience and make judgements about my encounters?"

"I'm not trying to say you didn't have a wonderful time. It sounds as though you did. All I am saying is that I have known Jim for many years. The fellow you describe is not the person I know."

"Well, I think you're being pretty narrow-minded to say I didn't meet your friend just because the fellow I met doesn't sound anything like him."

Such an exchange would sound rather ridiculous in the "real world." But, when it comes to god-talk (theo-logy), our discourse tends to get rather mushy and vacuous, what a philosophy professor of mine once called "artless, seeming language." And, yet, this is the tenor of much of the god-talk of our day. Any attempt to make a statement about the exact nature of God, or of The Faith, is hooted down as being judgmental, hierarchical, or ill-motivated.

The individualistic and relativistic intellectual and spiritual climate of our day reflects a crisis of authority. In that sense, it is not unlike the situation that faced the 16th century reformers. The centuries-old reliance on the See of Rome to see them through theological quandaries had been abruptly severed. What was the source of authority to be in the brave new world the reformers were discovering/inventing? It quickly became incumbent upon them to create clear, concise, and public statements about their core convictions and from whence their authority derived. The time for the Articles had arrived.

Discussion Questions

1) Complete this sentence: "God is . . . " Give some Scriptural support for your proposition.

2) Should religious discourse be different from other forms of discourse? Why or why not?

3) Why do you think so many people object to objectivity in the realm of religious discourse?

4) Is it possible to state a religious conviction with authority and conviction and not *appear to be* arrogant and/or judgmental? How?

Why Bother with the Articles at this Time & Place in the Life of the Anglican Church?

In religion, as in . . . . everything else, comfort is the one thing you cannot get by looking for it. If you look for truth, you may find comfort in the end: If you look for comfort you will not get either comfort or truth, only soft soap and wishful thinking to begin with and, in the end, despair.

C. S. Lewis

As we have used an ancient litmus test (Scripture, Tradition, and Reason) to demonstrate the essential validity of the Articles, we now turn to a current paradigm to explore their relevance and future applicability. It has become common in business and church contexts to analyze situations using a four-fold approach commonly referred to by its acronym, SWOT (Strengths, Weaknesses, Opportunities, Threats) Analysis. We will now use this helpful and concise matrix to muse upon the Articles.

Strengths

What strengths do the Articles bring to the current psycho/socio/theo-logical situation? Quite simply, they are concise, time-tested and accurate statements of historic Anglicanism. They have been brooded over, fussed over, tinkered with and fine-tuned by generations of faithful men and women.

They have proven themselves to be adaptable to a variety of cultures and times. They are moderate in that they are "patient" of both Catholic and Protestant interpretation, but still uncompromisingly affirm the Truth of the Gospel. They relieve the liturgy of carrying a burden for which it was never designed, that of articulating in a few words the essential truths of the "doctrine of Christ as this church has received them."

In 1842, after his plans to become a member of Parliament were frustrated, the twenty-six year old John Charles Ryle was ordained to the Anglican priesthood. He became Bishop of Liverpool in 1880 and held the post until his death in 1900. In the later part of the 19th century, in the wake of the Oxford Movement, the question of just what makes for a "good churchman" was a hot topic in England. Bishop Ryle, an articulate and well-written spokesman for Anglicanism and the Articles, saw the two as integrally related. Shortly before his selection for the episcopate, the soon-to-be Bishop Ryle wrote these words:

> The subject of this paper may, at first sight, seem dull and uninteresting. But in fact, this is not so, for there are few things as important as the Thirty-nine Articles, about which the Churchman should hold clear and correct opinions. Legal documents of all sorts are, to the general reader, most unattractive reading; but they are extremely important. This applies just as much to the Articles of Religion, which, in one sense, are the backbone of the Church of England.
>
> Further, I assert most emphatically that in the Articles, the Church of England has provided a test of true Churchmanship. Many and varied are the definitions of true Churchmanship. But it is not enough to define a true churchman as one who attends services every Sunday. There are many like this, knowing much about everything else, but yet completely ignorant of the doctrines of Christianity.
>
> Nor is 'Earnestness' a qualification for true Churchmanship. There have been many really earnest people opposed to Christianity. Earnestness may show a man has a lot of energy, but it does not prove him to be a true Churchman.
>
> In fact, none of the many definitions given is adequate to describe a true Churchman. But an honest examination of the Thirty-nine Articles of Religion forms a test which any man can

understand, and shows who is the best, truest and most genuine Churchman.

I think that no church on earth has a better Confession of Faith. Nothing can compare with the fulness, boldness, clarity, brevity, moderation and wisdom of the Articles of the Church of England.

I do say, and will show, that the Articles and not the Prayer Book are the first test of a true Churchman.

It is unreasonable to set up a book of devotion [by which he was referring to the BCP] as a better test of Churchmanship than a confession of faith. Prayers are not cold, dogmatic statements of doctrine.

Today [in 1877], anyone who is really positive and says "This is true, that is false" is sure to be called narrow, bigoted, uncharitable, or 'party.' But I shall always maintain that to call someone extreme or party because his views are in harmony with the Articles is not just, fair, nor reasonable, nor even common sense.

If the relevant acts were repealed and the Articles thrown out, then a churchman could be anything or everything.[66]

It is amazing how true his words are, even today. The Anglican Church would be well served to read, mark, learn, and inwardly digest them.

Weaknesses

No one argues that the Articles are perfect. For example, there is only one quote from our Lord (and that a fairly negative one). There is no mention of the Christian's hope.

Perhaps, the main weakness of the Articles is that they are perceived to be too time-bound to be relevant today. That is to be expected of any document written in time and place. The same could be said for the Scriptures. A proper hermeneutic handles this weakness.

---

66 Ryle, John Charles, "The Thirty-nine Articles." Reprinted and exerpted from his book *Knots Untied* printed in 1877. The reprint was issued in 1960.

Granted, the language is sometimes confusing and archaic. As we have shown, this is easily remedied.

It is also true that the issues today are not the same as they were in the 16th century. True. All the more reason to affirm the Articles and bring them up to date. David Broughton Knox has argued that we view the Articles as "incomplete." All would agree the Articles contain statements that are no longer quite as relevant in the year 2001 as they were in the year 1571, (or even in 1801) but that does not mean that those statements are untrue. Unless these few time-bound statements can be shown to be untrue, they should be retained. The Articles need to be added to in relevant, faithful ways. Issues such as sexuality, the role of women, responses to the challenges represented by mission work in the third world, etc. need explication.

In summary the Articles are incomplete in the same sense that the ecumenical creeds are also incomplete: for example, they say nothing of the Bible, anthropology, the sanctifying work of the Holy Spirit, etc. The Articles, like the creeds, cannot ultimately be judged by what they omitted but by what they affirmed.

Opportunities

Five forces are operating in the late 20th century in America, Europe, and indeed all over the world. These five forces are not new. They have marked the spirit of many ages of man. They were largely present in the first century when Christianity was birthed (though in a form that requires some thought to discern). They were present in the 16th century and helped propel and shape the Great Reformation that birthed the Anglican Church. They were present at the end of the 18th century at the founding of America and the "new" Protestant Episcopal Church in the United States. And, they are present today. They are secularism, spiritual renewal, episcopal dysfunction, sectarianism, and pluralism. In the past, the Church has wisely chosen to respond to these five forces through increased emphasis on witness, mission, and evangelism AND through a reaffirmation of its core convictions. We have that opportunity today. As the 1990's Episcopal Church's Decade of Evangelism draws to a close, it would be wise to enter a decade of theological reflection and refinement.

Secularism

The growth of secularism can be defined as the increasing tendency for people of faith to look outside the church, and The Faith, for answers and authority. This tendency was manifested at the very core of the "Enlightenment" that formed the intellectual background for the American Revolution much as the Renaissance had done for the Reformation.

Now, almost 200 years later, the seeds of secularism sowed in the soil of America by its "enlightened" founders have come to fruition. While still maintaining a veneer of religiosity, the average late 20th century American finds the church increasingly irrelevant and unreliable. "Up until about 1985, about two Americans in three expressed high confidence in the church or organized religion, and usually placed it ahead of institutions from the secular world. Then, there began a series of events that led to widespread disillusionment with organized religion. . . . The low point in confidence in the church was reached in 1989, when only a bare majority of 52 percent of Americans still had a great deal or quite a lot of confidence in it."[67]

In 1988, for the first time in the history of polling, the clergy were not the most respected profession. In that year, pharmacists, in their starched white vestments, dispensing the peace that passes understanding, overtook the clergy and have held on ever since. Why? Could it be that the pharmacy counter is replacing the communion rail as the place to find a humble, available authority figure offering healing and hope? In fact, ratings of clergy respectability have dropped further and faster than any other group in the last ten years.[68]

Christian clergy have been blessed to have a "vocation" that is congruent and integrated with their "profession" (in the fin-

---

67 The Princeton Religion Research Center, "Religion in America: 1992-1993," p. 60.

68 Ibid., p. 62.

est sense that their "calling" grows out of what they "profess"). Christian clergy are called to be "theologians," people who have been set apart to speak to other people about God (*theos logos*). It would clearly trivialize the calling of a clergyperson to reduce that calling to oratory or prose. It would equally compromise it to disregard the cognitive, didactic, and kerygmatic[69] portion of that ministry.

Yet, as our collective discomfort with, and disdain for, propositional truth has grown, Anglican clergy have tended to see their vocation not primarily as "professional theologians" but as amateur thespians and therapists. The temptation now is to define their individual ministries (and The Ministry) primarily in terms of liturgy and counseling rather than teaching and leading.

Paul admonished Timothy: "*What you heard from me, keep as the pattern of sound teaching, with faith and love in Christ Jesus. Guard the good deposit that was entrusted to you — guard it with the help of the Holy Spirit who lives in us*" (II Timothy 1:13-14). While only the bishop's ordination vows include a charge to "guard the faith," it is important to remember that Timothy was not even a "proto-bishop" when Paul encouraged him to see guarding sound doctrine as one of his "callings." And, at the risk of being flip, it is important to note that Paul's charge cited at the beginning of this paper did not say "Watch your life and rubrics closely." We are in danger of mirroring our culture, confusing orthopraxy (right actions, though not in a moral sense) with orthodoxy (right beliefs).

Americans may make a show of religion, but when it comes to finding truth for their troubles, they turn to the medical professional. When they are looking for objective truth they turn to the university, or Hollywood celebrities, not the Church. While there is a swing back to the metaphysical (New Age), it is not a swing back to anything resembling theologically informed worship. A naive drift toward eastern and dualistic categories form the presuppositional base of much that is happening in the "secular" world that surrounds our churches.

---

69 The "kerygma" is the Gospel proclaimed.

How would reaffirming the Articles help the Church deal with the challenges of Secularism? Questions raised by prayer in schools, sex education in the classroom, the tax and liability status of churches and religious institutions, Supreme Court rulings on moral issues, the right *vis a vis* the responsibility to bear arms (or to resist the taking up of arms), etc. require that Christians formulate a thoughtful and theological position on how the Church relates to the secular institutions that surround it.

(A) Primarily, we affirm that doctrine does have existential consequences, that "sweet, pleasant, and unspeakable comfort" (Article XVII) can be found in consistency of conviction, not just chemistry. "As a man thinketh . . . so is he." (B) Second, a reaffirmation of the Articles would reaffirm our presuppositional base, from which we can speak prophetically to a culture that is consciously distancing itself from us. We must recapture the verity that "conviction" regarding sin (personal and corporate) is not primarily a *feeling* of guilt, it is being "convicted" of one's real guilt relative to an objectively articulated standard. The Ten Commandments come to mind as an example of articulated, propositional truth. (C) Finally, the Articles help inform our consciences *vis a vis* the state and the limits of its legitimate claims on our lives and property.

Spiritual Renewal

Spiritual renewal, may be defined as an intangible but observable intensification of people's activities and understanding as it relates to the things of God. Almost by definition, it was self-evident during the Reformation of the 16th century. People across Europe and England were experiencing the Scriptures and liturgies in their own languages. New forms of religious expression were being welcomed and people were participating in the church in ways either undreamed of or unlawful even a few decades earlier. That same spirit of renewal was evident at the dawn of the 19th century and is much in evidence today.

The Articles were established by the Episcopal Church in 1801. That same year, Methodist Bishop Francis Asbury paused long enough in New York to send a message back to his colleagues in England. "He spoke glowingly of the hundreds of gospel ministers under his charge, of the 8,273 new members added during the last year, and of the pervasive sense that God's work was accelerating at an unprecedented rate." He delighted in "the rousing success of the American camp meeting. Describing the 'overwhelming power' of the four-day meeting . . . (he) found the level of activity so intense, with 'weeping on all sides,' that he was unable to sleep for the duration."

The Great Awakening had done a great deal of good — uniting the colonies and, thus, laying the foundation for the American Revolution — but it also fostered an anti-institutional and (in some quarters) anti-theological sentiment. During and after the Great Awakening "major non-Anglican religious groups also were being drawn together to resist Anglican encroachments."[70] It not only produced a backlash against institutional Christianity, it also tended to turn people against doctrinal Christianity. When one has "enthusiasm," theology and doctrine seem dry rations indeed, "flat tranquility against passion; dry leaves against the whirlwind; the weight of gunpowder against its kindled force."[71]

In such a milieu, *any* theology was suspect, especially any form of Calvinism — even the mild Calvinism of the Articles. But the populist religious movements did not attack Calvinism as if Arminianism or Lutheranism were the preferred rendering of scholastic theology. Instead, the attacks were directed against forms of Christianity that eschewed the palpable presence of God and were "preoccupied with theology."[72] Yet, there is a difference between being "preoccupied with theology" and having a theology at all and Anglicans knew it.

Americans had become as skeptical of skepticism as they were of theology. "Enlightenment critics had blown and blown with all their might against the house of Scripture, but that house had

---

70   Hudson, p. 100.

71   Hatch, Nathan, *The Democratization of American Christianity*, p. 46.

72   Ibid., p. 174.

not fallen. In the first generation of the 19th century, far more Americans knew Moses and Paul than Bacon and Voltaire — and knew them far better."[73] Americans, a people alive with vision and vigor, intuitively sought what Jonathan Edwards had called "religious affections."

During the first decade of the 19th century, the American frontier, a wilderness of biblical proportions, claimed the imaginations of the people in the pews. What these frontier-intoxicated Americans wanted was a spiritual experience that was as vigorous and majestic as the vast, unexplored, and untamed frontier that energized America's vision of itself. Who wants to read Luther and Calvin when one can read Lewis and Clark?

The leaders of the Episcopal Church knew from historical experience that enthusiasms would fade. Without a theological "infrastructure" to give meaning to the experiences, any gains in holiness and godliness would be fleeting. Thus, it was against this anti-theological/anti-doctrinal background that the Episcopal Church raised the flag of theology and doctrine by embracing the Articles — not just a bold move, but a wise one. A similar bold and wise commitment is called for today.

How would reaffirming the Articles help the Church deal with the challenges of spiritual renewal? Once again, American Christians and Americans in general are skeptical of skeptics. They are hungry to believe, willing to follow and invest in anyone or anything that offers the confidence of conviction. The last several decades have been years of renewal within the Church. The "Jesus" movement of the sixties and the charismatic movement of the seventies and eighties have become part of "mainstream" institutions in contemporary Christianity. The "enthusiasm" that resulted has pushed outward from the "traditions" of the past. A spiritual frontier has opened that has captured the imaginations of the people in our pews. Reaffirming the Articles will reaffirm the fact that theology is a guide to experience. Hooker's three-legged stool has not sprouted a fourth and decisive leg. New experiences must be interpreted in light of established truth.

---

73   Gaustad, Edwin S., *Faith of Our Fathers*, pp. 129, 130.

One of the first things any undergraduate philosophy major learns is that "You can't get an ought from an is." All experience is "true" in the sense that it exists, but all interpretations of experience are not "Truth." There must be a standard that exists outside the experience by which the experience is judged.

Episcopal Dysfunction

It had been episcopal dysfunction (the inability of bishops to give effective oversight and leadership) at the highest level that had caused Henry VIII's actions in the first place. The Pope's inability to loose himself from the control of England's political enemies, added to the legendary abuses of the medieval bishops, had made the episcopacy an institution with many enemies.[74] The American Episcopacy at the beginning of the 19th century was a confused and dispirited lot. The Episcopacy today faces many of the same problems.

The word "episcopal" is the Greek word for 'bishop." It literally means "over-seer." Early in its history, the newly independent American branch of the Anglican Church chose to be identified by reference to its form of government. (Other examples of this would be the "Congregationalists" and the "Presbyterians" — presbyter being the Greek word for "elder.") Thus, the veracity, tenacity, efficacy, and integrity of the bishop's office is a vital part of who Anglican Christians claim to be. For many American Anglicans, therefore, to even entertain questions and concerns about the episcopacy is to raise corresponding questions and concerns about the very core of what it means to be a Christian. It is a little like Lutherans questioning whether Luther was really all that clever or Baptists wondering aloud if baptism is really all that important. It is very unsettling.

Therefore, the subject of episcopal dysfunction is one delicately, but necessarily, approached. Ever since Richard Hooker

---

74 Barbara Tuchman has done a masterful job of portraying the medieval episcopal dysfunction in her book *The March of Folly.*

adumbrated the three-legged stool of Scripture, Tradition, and Reason, Anglicans have stood apart from the majority of Protestantism by affirming the *primacy* of Scripture as opposed to *sola scriptura*. Coincident with the lamentable decline in our collective convictions regarding the veracity of Scripture, one senses a move away from the primacy of Scripture and toward the "primacy" of the episcopate.

For example, in 1982, the Episcopal Church began to call the Presiding Bishop a "Primate" for the first time in the Church's 200 year history. The debate over the issue was so stormy that it had to be cut off so a vote could be taken. Some would argue that a name change is meaningless as regards function. Well, if that is the case, why bother doing it in the first place? In this light it is interesting that the American Church has decided to reduce the term of this office from 12 years to 9.

All this must be taken in light of the meeting of the House of Bishops that occurred at Kanuga in March, 1992. They had come together to address some of the problems they were experiencing. Their verdict on themselves: according to Bishop FitzSimons Allison, "People agreed it was dysfunctional. Liberals and conservatives alike — it was unanimous."[75] "Bishops expressed an eagerness to heal some of the dysfunctions of the house so that the bishops could provide some theological leadership for the church."[76] While one is prayerfully hopeful that this will occur, grass-roots Episcopalians are mindful of the current dysfunction and distrustful as a result. Again, the situation in 1801 is instructive.

In 1801, Bishop Samuel Provoost, "relinquished his episcopal duties, convinced that the church would 'die out with the old families.'"[77] Provoost had been one of the founders of the Episcopal Church, a man who had served as chaplain to the Congress and to the Senate, and who had been the third Presiding Bishop of the new church from 1792-1795. Thus, not too long

---

75 Bp. C. FitzSimons Allison, *United Voice*, p. 2.

76 Solheim, James, "Special Meeting of Bishops Expresses Determination to Make Radical Changes," p. 9.

77 Hudson, p. 117.

after the Church had scoured the British Empire trying to lay claim to Apostolic succession, and at a time when the young Church needed leaders with apostolic vision, one of the most prominent American "apostles" was calling it quits. And he was not alone. "The effort [of getting the Episcopal Church established] had exhausted the energy of many in the church. The aging leadership began to die, and new leaders were not immediately forthcoming."[78]

"In Virginia, no more than forty of the one hundred seven Episcopal parishes existing in 1784 were able to support ministers during the decade of 1802-1811. . . Bishop James Madison (1790-1812) ordained only one deacon for the entire state in the first decade of the new century and witnessed only three young men in training for the priesthood. By 1805 Madison was so despondent that he went into seclusion, leaving the church too weak and badly organized to contemplate the challenge of moving forward and going West. . . "[79] One historian noted that "for many years after its organization in 1789, the Protestant Episcopal Church more 'closely resembled an executor settling the bankrupt estate of the old Anglican establishment than the heir of a rich and vital religious tradition.'"[80]

America had opted, unlike England, for a written constitution, to be a nation of "laws, not men." Americans had just thrown out the scepter, they were reluctant to keep the miter. According to the *St. James Chronicle*, "stamping and episcopizing" were commonly regarded as "different branches of the same plan of power."[81] John Adams had warned ominously of "a direct and formal design to enslave America."[82] "'I know of no divine authority,' Adams wrote, 'for Lords Popes or Lords Cardinals or Lords Bishops . . . All that any of these 'Lords' have been good

---

78   Prichard, Robert, *A History of the Episcopal Church*, p. 97.

79   Hatch, p. 60.

80   Ibid., p. 60.

81   Hudson, p. 91.

82   Ibid., pp. 100, 101.

for is 'to deliver a man over to Satan to be buffeted.'"[83] The American Revolution "was more anticlerical than most historians recognize."[84]

Yet, in the face of all this, the American Anglican Church embraced the name "Episcopal" at a time when people not only knew what it meant, but didn't like what it meant. But, they also embraced the Articles, saying, in essence, that like the new country it called home, the new Episcopal Church would be a church of written doctrines, not only of men. Bishops came and bishops went, but the parishioners could be assured that the church rested on a body of agreed-upon truth that even the layman could read while he sat in the pew. Thus, the American Church chose to retain the episcopacy at a time when the episcopacy itself was clearly dysfunctional and unpopular. Yet, the Church also chose to set a hedge around the episcopacy, by affirming its reliance on confessional unity and shared conviction.

Unfortunately, many of the "ordinaries" of today seem to be taking their orders from the prevailing culture instead of Scripture, Tradition, or Reason, let alone a shared confessional theology. For example, during the current debate on Christian sexuality, according to the Episcopal magazine *The Living Church*, Bishop Orris Walker (Long Island) argued that regional differences were the root of the problem. "Over half the people in my diocese are single," he said. "If you ask me to go home to Brooklyn and Queens and run this by them, it ain't gonna fly." *Lex Volare — Lex Credendi? (The law of flying is the law of believing?)* Bishop Terence Kelshaw rightly reminded his colleague, "The Church can't do its theology based on what goes on in the streets."[85] *Lex Via — Lex Credendi?* Is the "law of the streets" really the "law of believing"?

Of course it isn't. And no responsible Christian would say that it should be. Nor do the Articles speak directly to the issue of sexual morality. Further, anyone who has read Shakespeare knows that sexual immorality was not unknown in 16th century

---

83 Gaustad, *Faith of Our Fathers*, p. 95.

84 Ibid., p. 110.

85 Steenson, Jeffrey, *The Living Church*, p. 9.

England. Yet, the crucial question for our purpose is not, "What
should be the Anglican theology of sexuality?" but rather "How
does the Anglican Church do theology?" The relative anarchy
within the episcopacy makes the need for an objective standard
all the more critical.[86]

One is reminded of the Council at Jerusalem, (see *Acts 15*)
when missionaries to foreign cultures brought back their witnesses to be tempered by the wisdom of the apostles. But, it is
important to note that one of the few things on which the Church
would *not* flex was sexual immorality. One cannot imagine a
more sexually immoral place to be a missionary than ancient
Corinth. Yet the early Church said that its theology must guide
ethics, no matter how unpopular it may be in the streets of
Corinth — or Queens.

How would reaffirming the Articles help the Church with
the challenges of episcopal dysfunction? It would reaffirm that

---

86 While the Articles themselves do not speak to the issue of human sexuality, they
do underline and endorse the important concept that The Church "be a witness
and keeper of Holy Writ" (Article XX). In that context, and with that authority in
mind, the decision of the Anglican bishops gathered at Lambeth in 1998 is significant. At that historic meeting, Anglican bishops from around the world overwhelm-
ingly (526 to 70) endorsed the following resolution which clearly upholds the biblical, traditional, and reasonable standard of human sexuality.

Resolution 1.10 of the Lambeth Conference
Human Sexuality
This Conference:

I.   commends to the Church the sub-section report on human sexuality;

II.   in view of the teaching of Scripture, upholds faithfulness in marriage between
a man and a woman in lifelong union, and believes that abstinence is right
for those who are not called to marriage;

III. recognizes that there are among us persons who experience themselves as
having a homosexual orientation. Many of these are members of the Church
and are seeking the pastoral care, moral direction of the Church, and God's
transforming power for the living of their lives and the ordering of relation-
ships. We commit ourselves to listen to the experience of homosexual persons and we wish to assure them that they are loved by God and that all
baptized, believing and faithful persons, regardless of sexual orientation, are
full members of the Body of Christ;

IV.   while rejecting homosexual practice as incompatible with Scripture, calls on
all our people to minister pastorally and sensitively to all irrespective of sexual

ours is a Church of doctrines, not men. We have historic precedent and a basis for discipline. One of only two places where the word "Church" appears on the lips of Jesus[87] is in the context of discipline. The reformers argued that one of the marks of the true Church was the exercise of Godly *discipline*. The episcopacy is admittedly dysfunctional, divided, and either unwilling or unable to discipline its own members. Without discipline there can be no discipleship. A reaffirmation of the Articles would reaffirm the primacy of Scripture (Articles VI & XX). It is the only place where the canonical books of the Scripture are named. It is the Articles that remind us that one of the cardinal convictions of Protestantism is that "councils do err" and that God has not spoken *ex cathedra* every time the Church speaks *ex convention* (Articles XX & XXI).

Sectarianism

Sectarianism refers to groups that voluntarily separate from the main body for reasons of theological conviction, but who see themselves as representing the "true" Church over and against the Church they left. This force was most clearly manifested in England in the presence of the Puritans and

---

orientation and to condemn the irrational fear of homosexuals, violence within marriage and any trivialisation and commercialisation of sex:

V. cannot advise the legitimizing or blessing same sex unions nor ordaining those involved in same gender unions;

VI. requests the Primates and the ACC to establish a means of monitoring the work done on the subject of human sexuality in the communion and to share statements and resources among us.

VII. notes the significance of the Kuala Lumpur Statement on Human Sexuality and the concerns expressed in Resolutions IV.26, V.1, V.10, V.23 and V.35 on the authority of Scripture in matters of marriage and sexuality and asks the Primates and the ACC to include them in their monitoring process.

87 The current writer is well aware that there exists a so-called "higher" critical approach which questions whether Jesus himself actually spoke this exact word. Those who hold this position would maintain that the word "church" simply did not exist in the time of Jesus and that it was placed on his lips by the early church and/ or the author of the text. For our purposes, however, whether the word was that of Jesus or the early church itself, it still speaks volumes about the relative importance of discipline to the church community.

the Anabaptists. Initially, these groups challenged the ecclesiastical and theological traditions of the Church from within. In the end, each ended up separating and founding new ecclesiastical and theological traditions.

In 1801, the Methodists were only 17 years old as an American Church. But by 1850 there were "far more Methodist churches than those of Congregationalists, Presbyterians, Episcopalians, and Lutherans combined."[88] As an Anglican priest, Wesley had assented to the Articles. But when he thought better of it, he did not say such a disagreement was "unimportant" or encourage his followers not to "concern themselves" with the differences and simply concentrate on their experience of spiritual renewal. Wesley sought to express his convictions in propositional form. In 1784, while still an Anglican clergyman, he produced his own *Twenty-Five Articles*.[89] Wesley never chose to leave the Church of England, but when one examines his articles in light of their Episcopal and/or Anglican counterparts, the issues that precipitated the eventual separation become very clear. (Such a simple exercise would have helped my former Methodist friend a great deal and saved him no small frustration over the years.) The mere presence of the Articles did not preserve unity with the "methodist" Anglicans in the 18th century any more than it had with the "puritan" Anglicans in the 16th. *But*, if there is ever to be a reconciliation of our "unhappy divisions," for which all Christians pray, the starting point for such reconciliation is a clear statement of what separates us. The Articles still provide that.

In recent years, the Anglican Church has begun to feel cracks in the foundations. Sectarianism, in the form of various splinter groups and attempts to form a non-geographic province, have threatened traditional understandings of church unity.

How would reaffirming the Articles help the Church with the challenges of sectarianism? Because of their inherent moderation and the fact that they were apparently intended to provide a basis for the comprehension within a national church of

---

88 Gaustad, *Faith of Our Fathers*, p. 123.

89 Harmon, Nolan Bailey, "John Wesley and the Articles of Religion," p. 280.

the various shades of mainstream Protestantism,[90] they still have the potential to unite various factions within the Church.

One of the five largest churches in a southern diocese recently left The Episcopal Church to join the Charismatic Episcopal Church. This church is now planting a "mission" church in my neighborhood. Thus, the "Charismatic Episcopal" church will hoist its steeple next to the "American Episcopal" church which moved into town about five years ago. When people ask "Why are there three 'different' Episcopal churches in this one, little neighborhood? What is the difference?" We can't just say, "They're schismatics, avoid them." We must be able to articulate our unique convictions and commitments; and those run deeper than which hymnal or prayer book we use. The differences in our liturgies were driven by, informed by, and formed by, our various doctrines. The American Episcopal Church, for example, uses the 1928 *BCP* not just because of the solemnity of Elizabethan English, but also because of the sacramental theology implicit in the liturgy. The prayer book of the Reformed Episcopal Church does not use the word "priest" to refer to ordained persons because, in their convictions, to do so would violate the protestant doctrine of the "priesthood of all believers."

Do we simply "compete"[91] with each other based on the cleanliness of *our* nursery, the dynamism of *our* youth program, the fact that *w e* have a pipe organ (or a band, or a character generator, or a . . . you name it)? Do we simply stand outside and holler that we were here first and they are not being *real* Anglicans? I submit that the best, most helpful, and most honest way to deal with Sectarianism is to clearly and concisely state exactly *what* it is that we believe and to what, and to *Whom* we are committed.

Pluralism

Pluralism is the acceptance of the presence of many sects without any real hope or expectation that a) there will be any

---

90 Avis, Paul, "What is 'Anglicanism?'," p. 418.

91 If the concept of "competition" offends, the reader is invited to substitute the word "differentiate," and to see below the discussion on "Pluralism."

union or b) that any one group represents The Truth as regards its differences with any other group. By the end of the 16th century, Europe was a self-consciously heterogenous patchwork of various competing Protestant and Roman Catholic sentiments. The American spiritual landscape at the beginning of the 19th century was an even more colorful quilt of various religious persuasions and convictions. Religious America today is even more a mosaic than a melting pot.

In 1801, "Grumpy Church of England Missionary Charles Woodmason" tried to preach to his modest congregation. Much to his chagrin, "Scottish Presbyterians had hired lawless ruffians to insult him — which they did, telling him they wanted no 'Damned Black Gown Sons of Bitches' among them . . .. Once he counted fifty-seven dogs that they set to fighting under the windows where he held services." In America, pluralism meant that "free enterprise had come to the world of religion."[92]

Pluralism is exhilarating within limits. But "the bewildering array of religious options in the new nation heightened the sense that something had gone awry."[93] America had produced an almost level playing field, but there also seemed to be no recognizable rules, except maybe *caveat emptor*. How were Episcopalians to relate to this array gone awry? To whom does one extend the right hand of fellowship and to whom does one extend a gospel tract?[94]

It has been said that Christianity started out in Palestine as a fellowship, it moved to Greece and became a philosophy, it moved to Italy and became an institution, it moved to Europe and became a culture, it came to America and became an enterprise. While that truth has always seemed unseemly, it has never seemed more true. Words like "marketing" are becoming part of the Episcopal dictionary.

Between the years 1534 (when Henry VIII first broke with Rome) and 1571 (when the Articles were finally adopted), no less than eight separate sets of "articles" defining the "new faith"

---

92 Martin, Marty, *Pilgrims in Their Own Land*, pp. 127, 128.

93 Hatch, p. 169.

94 Bebbington, David, *Evangelicalism in Modern Britain*, p. 338.

were articulated.[95] At first, the new faith looked a lot like the old; the main difference being ecclesiology not theology. But, ultimately, the driving force of the English Reformation was theology, not ecclesiology. Over those four decades, a unique approach to the Christian Faith emerged. Just one year after the break with Rome, the King's chaplain, Thomas Starkey, wrote "An Exhortation to Unity and Obedience" in which he commends a "midway between papism and radicalism."[96] How was this "unity and obedience" to be achieved? The Church apparently believed that a significant part of the answer was in establishing some limited form of doctrinal conformity. The full title of the Articles is instructive at this point: *Articles Agreed upon by the Archbishops and Bishops of both Provinces, and the whole Clergy in the Convocation holden at London in the year 1562, for the avoiding of diversities of opinions and for the establishing of Consent touching true religion.*[97] [emphasis added] Thus, one way the Church sought to achieve unity and articulate its uniqueness *and its catholicity* was through the careful, deliberate, and deliberated articulation and promulgation of specific theological convictions.

Reflecting on the pluralism of America in the early 19th century, Alexis de Tocqueville noted that the genius of American religion was in "respecting all democratic tendencies not absolutely contrary to herself, and by making use of several of them for her own purposes, Religion sustains a successful struggle with that spirit of individual independence which is her most dangerous opponent."[98] "The first object, and one of the principle advantages of religion is to furnish to each of these fundamental questions a solution which is at once *clear, precise, intelligible to the mass of mankind, and lasting.*"[99] [emphasis added] Perplexed Episcopalians turned to the Articles and found in them clarity amidst confusion, precision amidst ambiguity and obfusca-

---

95 Wright, Tom, "Doctrine Declared," p. 122.

96 Spitz, Lewis, *The Protestant Reformation*, p. 156.

97 Toon, Peter, "The Articles and Homilies," pp. 135-136.

98 de Tocqueville, Alexis, Richard Heffner, ed., *Democracy in America*, p. 155.

99 Ibid., p. 151.

tion, intelligence amidst rhetoric, and endurance amidst fadism: in short, just the sort of religion de Tocqueville commended.

It is true that the forces of spiritual renewal unleashed during the Great Awakening had created a façade of unity based on shared enthusiasms. But by the early 19th century, reality had reared its ugly head. "While the rhetoric of unity was omnipresent in American churches, centrifugal forces had never been more acute. . . . Between 1800 and 1830 a wildly diverse religious culture made both denominational identity and authority fragile creations. Outside of the face-to-face discipline exercised in local churches, many denominations maintained their authority only by seldom exercising it."[100]

If early 19th century America presented a daunting array of options, late 20th century America is even more diverse. "In the 1950's, only 4% of the average congregations' members had grown up in another denomination. Now that figure is over 40%. Churchgoers have largely lost the common heritage that used to unify congregations. There is greater diversity of belief within most congregations today than there used to be between denominations."[101] According to "Religion in America: 1992-1993," a report prepared by the Princeton Religion Research Center, Episcopalians were, *per capita*, the largest group of denominational "switchers" of any communion, switching at a rate much higher than any other denomination.[102] The most prominent reason giving for switching was a preference for "the religious stance of another church."[103] When asked what mainline denominations can do to strengthen their position in the pluralistic world of the late 20th century, Lyle Schaller offered several bits of advice at a conference in August, 1994. Included in that was the advice "Do not apologize for a distinctive belief system."[104]

---

100   Hatch, p. 63.

101   *Net Result,* February, 1993. Quoted in *The Pastor's Weekly Briefing,* September 23, 1994.

102   Hudson, Winthrop, *Religion in America,* p. 38.

103   Ibid.

104   Miller, Kevin A., *Christianity Today,* p. 72.

How would reaffirming the Articles help the Church with the challenges of Pluralism? (A) Because the bedrock basics of The Christian Faith are there articulated in Article VIII, a reaffirmation of the Articles would help answer the question of what constitutes a "true" church, one with whom we as Anglicans can share at least fellowship, if not full communion. Articles XXV - XXXI answer the question of those with whom Anglicans may share a sacramental ministry. Articles XIX - XXI articulate the nature, power, and limits of true churches. (B) A reaffirmation (*and subsequent revision, see below*) of the Articles would clearly articulate *not just "Anglican"* distinctives, but *our* distinctive "Anglican" distinctives.

As the nascent Episcopal Church was learning to survive, compete, and, yes, flourish in the Pluralism of a "new world," the Articles were the collective basis for discussion, dialogue, and decisions with other Christian bodies. They provided Episcopalians with a rule and guide that was at once solidly Protestant in theology yet moderate in application.

Threats

There are two major threats to the Articles today: plain, old garden-variety apathy and a perceived change in the way the Church understands truth claims.

First, and most pernicious, is the indignity of indifference. Anglican scholar John Macquarrie's *Principles of Christian Theology*, the standard theology text at many Anglican theological seminaries, never even mentions the Articles. Massey Shepherd, in his 1952 contribution to the popular Episcopal Church's Teaching Series, *The Worship of the Church* only mentions the Articles once, and that in passing during a paragraph on confirmation.[105] In his seminal work, *The Oxford American Prayer Book Commentary*, (1950) he reprints the Articles and introduces them with a four-page commentary. While Marion Hatchett's *Commentary on the American Prayer Book* gives a good basic introduction to the Articles, one would have hoped for more depth in relating this seminal document to the current life of the Church.

---

105 Shepherd, Massey Hamilton, *The Worship of the Church*, p. 178.

The source of this indifference is rooted in a systemic antipathy to doctrine within the Anglican Church. As David Knox has observed, "The harsh things which are sometimes said about the Church of England's Thirty-nine Articles of Religion are symptomatic of the much more widespread dislike of doctrinal Christianity which has invaded the Church in our day."[106] That is why it is important to note that this book is not solely a defense of the Articles as they are currently configured. It is an apology for having Articles, period.

The inherent instability of relying solely on the liturgy and the episcopacy to carry the load of doctrinal clarity is becoming evident. Having rejected doctrinal articulations, liturgical revision and episcopal dysfunction have no corrective context, no court of appeals except public opinion and the verdict of history. Well, public opinion is screaming at the Episcopal Church in America. With a mere one percent of the American population, there are five times as many Americans who believe Elvis is still alive as there are Episcopalians.

The verdict of history will not be in for a while, but the early results are not encouraging. For a church that had such a colorful and exciting beginning, the future may hold a rather dull and lifeless demise if we do not soon adopt and apply some corrective measures to our lack of theological identity and definition.

Discussion Questions

1) While no one would say that popularity is any indication of truth, is it important for Christian denominations to take note of internal and/or external demographic trends?

2) Which of the five opportunities do you believe to offer the greatest challenge? The greatest potential rewards?

3) Is diversity and/or pluralism a value to be fostered or a variable to be controlled?

4) What are the best ways to maintain unity within diversity?

---

106   Knox, *Thirty-Nine Articles: The Historic Basis of the Anglican Faith*, p. 5.

∾ S·E·V·E·N ∾

A Commentary on the Articles

I think that no church on earth has a better Confession of Faith. Nothing can compare with the fulness, boldness, clarity, brevity, moderation and wisdom of the Articles of the Church of England.

Bishop J. C. Ryle

Articles of Religion: As established by the Bishops, the Clergy, and the Laity of the Protestant Episcopal Church in the United States of America, in Convention, on the twelfth day of September, in the Year of our Lord, 1801.

The reader should note well this introductory paragraph. It reminds us that the Articles were "established" at a specific place and time in the life of this Church. As was discussed above, the act of establishment was an intentional move that went beyond mere acceptance or acknowledgment. No other document in the history of the Church has ever been similarly "established." This unprecedented action was not done in a corner. Nor was it done by a special interest group within the Church. It was done in convention and by common consent of the Bishops, Clergy, and Laity of the Church.

The LORD reveals Himself as a God who works through generations. In His sovereignty, God has chosen to establish His covenant with families through the generations. This is how God revealed Himself to Abram. *"I will establish my covenant as an everlasting covenant between me and you and your descendants after you for the generations to come, to be your God and the God of your descendants after you" (Genesis 17:7).*

77

Anglicans who live during the dawn of a new millennium owe much to those faithful men and women who have gone before and on whose shoulders we collectively make our stand.

> **I. Of Faith in the Holy Trinity.** There is but one living and true God, everlasting, without body, parts, or passions; of infinite power, wisdom, and goodness; the Maker, and Preserver of all things both visible and invisible. And in unity of this Godhead there be three Persons, of one substance, power, and eternity; the Father, the Son, and the Holy Ghost.

As we examine each article in turn, the reader should note the repeated use of the words "true" and "truly." The framers of these Articles wanted to make certain that their readers knew they were not speaking metaphorically.

The first article focuses on God and the place He has consigned Himself in His universe. This is a classic apologetic that goes all the way back to Mars Hill and beyond. The Psalmist states boldly that it is the "fool" who says there is no God (*Psalm 14:1*) while the writer to the Hebrews reminds us that *"anyone who comes to him (God) must believe that he exists and that he rewards those who earnestly seek him"* (*Hebrews 11:6*).

When the Apostle Paul confronted a culture in which he could not assume that Jewish monotheism was the presumptive base, he began his defense of the Christian Faith by an eloquent and reasoned argument about the nature and attributes of God. (*See Acts 17 for Paul's address on Mars Hill, a.k.a. the Areopagus, and an excellent example of this type of apologetic.*)

In a passage from one of Paul's epistles, he makes it clear to his readers in Rome that certain aspects of God's nature can be readily apprehended by humankind. *". . .what may be known about God is plain to them, because God has made it plain to them. For since the creation of the world God's invisible qualities — his eternal power and divine nature — have been clearly seen, being understood from what has been made, so that men are without excuse"* (*Romans 1:19-20*).

Article I echoes Paul's point but then expands on it. Certainly, God's "infinite power" and His "wisdom" are evident in creation, what theologians have called "general revelation" because it is revealed to all people equally and in all of creation. But, the "goodness" of God can only ultimately be affirmed by seeing history through the lens of the Gospel of Christ. This is because without the cross of Christ, there is no irrefutable witness to God's goodness. While God's power and wisdom is displayed in mountain vistas, colorful sunsets, and the magnificence of space, the natural order (because it is fallen) is a rather mean place. Animals must forage for food, often consuming other life forms in the process. People die of awful diseases. Disasters come with a capriciousness that defies any ethic.

Jesus Himself said that the rain falls on the just and the unjust alike. The one time He had a chance to get God off the hook for a seemingly arbitrary disaster, He ignored the opportunity and issued a warning instead (see *Luke 13:1-5*). Yes, the stark truth is that it is only the Christian who can affirm the ultimate goodness of God based on anything other than sentimentality and wishful thinking . . . if you can call it thinking at all.

Unless a person has just finished a class in Aristotelian metaphysics, 99.9% of all modern people think of the word "substance" in images of . . . well . . . something "substantial". . . literally "some-*thing*." (To our minds, it seems almost oxymoronic to refer to a Spirit as "substantial," but that is what God is.) In this case, the word is used in an Aristotelian sense, not in a colloquial sense. When the Nicene Creed affirms that Jesus was of "one substance" with the Father, it did not mean that they were made of the same "stuff." It did not refer to "stuff" at all but the essential nature of an entity.[107]

Pantheism was not a burning issue in the 16th century, but the framers of the Articles still believed they needed to affirm the unity of God. How much more do we, living in an

---

107 Take, for example, the classic example of a triangle. Triangles come in many shapes and sizes, but they all share the essence of what it is to be a triangle. The actual lines on the paper are the "accidence," but the shape itself is the "substance." A more interesting and perplexing example is to try to articulate the substantial element of "color," without reference to any particular color.

We will meet this ancient but foundational epistemology (the study of how we know "what is") later when we discuss "transubstantiation."

age that is prone to pantheism and henotheism,[108] need to re-affirm the seminal truth God Himself gave to Moses so long ago and commanded him to "Hear it" — the *Shema Israel: "Hear, O Israel: The Lord our God, the Lord is one. Love the Lord your God with all your heart and with all your soul and with all your strength"* (*Deuteronomy 6:4-5*).

At this point, an honest question would be, how can a God Who commands passion, and Who defines His own creation (made in His image) as having parts, be described as without "passion" and/or "parts"? It obviously hinges on how we use those terms. What can it mean that God is without parts or passion? To say that God is "without parts" (*impartibilis* in Latin) means that, as a Spirit, God cannot be divided or dissected. His eternal nature is totally homogeneous, God has "integrity" in the purest sense of that term. He reveals Himself as a God *"with whom is no variableness, neither shadow of turning"* (*James 1:17 KJV*).

To say that God is "without passions" (*impassibilis* in Latin) means that He is incapable of being moved by anything other than His eternal will which is not to say that God is incapable of suffering or grieving, etc. For example, we are told that *"The Lord was grieved that he had made man on the earth, and his heart was filled with pain"* (*Genesis 6:6*).

We must hasten to add, however, that such biblical texts are not simply primitive anthropomorphisms meant to give a helping hand to less developed cultures on their wayward way toward the type of "sophisticated" discourse that fills most theological text books. These are actual expressions of how God actually relates to His world. I rejoice that being made in the image of God means that I am a person, just as He is personal.

The term "Trinity" is not found either in the Scriptures or the Creeds. The doctrine developed after the first century as a way to try to comprehend the complexity of God's Self-revelation, especially as it related to our redemption. Of course, it has confounded theologians for millennia. We will come to it again

---

108 "Pantheism" is the belief that *everything* ("pan") is god. "Henotheism" is a fancy word for a kind of relativism that affirms the existence of many gods while still affirming one as the best — a sort of cosmic "first among equals."

when we discuss the atonement. Until then, as a professor of mine once wryly observed, if you understand the Trinity, you've got it wrong.

> **II. Of the Word or Son of God, which was made very Man.** The Son, which is the Word of the Father, begotten from everlasting of the Father, the very and eternal God, and of one substance with the Father, took Man's nature in the womb of the blessed Virgin, of her substance: so that two whole and perfect Natures, that is to say, the Godhead and Manhood, were joined together in one Person, never to be divided, whereof is one Christ, very God, and very Man; who truly suffered, was crucified, dead, and buried, to reconcile his Father to us, and to be a sacrifice, not only for original guilt, but also for actual sins of men.

I had a professor once who said that *John 1:14, "the Word became flesh and dwelt among us,"* was the most important sentence in the history of the world. Paul reminds us that it is the doctrine of the incarnation, that God could take on human flesh and die on a cross, that is *"a stumbling block to Jews and foolishness to Gentiles"* (*I Corinthians 1:23*).

The Article reaffirms the classic Nicean formula that the Son is of one "substance" with the Father. It goes on to explicate the mystery of the incarnation in that the person of Jesus fully combined two "whole and perfect Natures, that is to say, the Godhead and Manhood, were joined in one Person." Because He was truly born of a virgin through the power of God's Spirit, Jesus was fully God *and* fully human. If it were not so, He could not have been the Savior. The doctrine of the Trinity turns on this point.

The Articles are unusual among formularies of the 16th century because they make the section on Christology (the study of the work of Christ) integral to "Theology." Articles II, III, and IV relate to the work of the second Person of the Trinity especially as they relate to His atoning work. By placing the articles about Christ's work in the section on the Godhead, the Articles rightly discern and proclaim that unless Christ was truly and fully God incarnate, His death — however noble and beautiful — was not an atonement. This is because, since the offense of sin was against the holiness of the Godhead, unless the Son is a full member of the Godhead, He could not embrace the penalty for that sin.

Think of it this way. Person A loans his car to person B. Person B wrecks the car. Person A has two choices, he can either say, "B, you wrecked my car, you pay for it," or he can say, "I forgive you, B, the cost of repairing the car. Go in peace." In the first case, B must pay the debt incurred by the transgression (wrecking the car). In the second case, the owner of the car embraces the debt and pays it himself. The car is not, somehow, magically fixed just because A was gracious to B — there is still a debt to be paid.

Here is where it gets a little tricky. Many Christians believe that what God (person A in our little story) did was go out and get an innocent third party (person C = Jesus Christ) and extract the price of the transgression from Him. Thus, B (the offender — that's us) is off the hook, A (the owner) gets his debt repaid and C (the innocent bystander) gets to suffer. You can see that this does not make sense unless C was also a legitimate partner in the transaction from the beginning. Jesus cannot forgive a debt that is not owed to *Him*. And that is what He did on the cross — He paid the debt of death (*"For the wages of sin is death,"* *Romans 6:23*) for those who incurred the debt. Since the debt was owed to the holy Godhead, only a member of the Godhead could erase (forgive) the debt. This is why Jesus' statement to the paralytic in *Mark 2:7* that his sins were forgiven provoked this very understandable reaction from the teachers of the law who were sitting there, *"Why does this fellow talk like that? He's blaspheming! Who can forgive sins but God alone?"* That was precisely the point Jesus was trying to make.

Attempts to understand the full complexity and magnificence of what happened on the cross inevitably find expression in the form of metaphor. Reconciliation is one of the great Pauline/Biblical metaphors for what Christ did on the cross. Some of the others are "justification," "redemption," "atonement," and "propitiation."

As any computerphile knows, the terms "justification" and "reconciliation" are to be found as buttons on many computer programs. This rather pedestrian use of these theological sounding terms gives us important clues as to their meaning. To "justify" something (like a margin in the text) is to bring it into alignment with a standard that has already been determined. The Scripture uses the image of a plumbline for the same purpose (see *Amos 7:7, 8*). By Christ's death we are declared to be justified, brought into alignment with God's standards. To use the helpful, if somewhat simplistic, summary "Justification means it is 'just as if' I had never sinned."

To "reconcile" (often used in financial programs) means to bring two things together so that they are compatible. When a financial ledger is "reconciled," it indicates that credits have been counted toward all applicable debit. See if you can follow Paul's use of this metaphor in *Romans 4:3-5 & 22-24*: *"What does the Scripture say? 'Abraham believed God, and it was credited to him as righteousness.' Now when a man works, his wages are not credited to him as a gift, but as an obligation. However, to the man who does not work but trusts God who justifies the wicked, his faith is credited as righteousness. . . . This is why 'it was credited to him as righteousness.' The words 'it was credited to him' were written not for him alone, but also for us, to whom God will credit righteousness — for us who believe in him who raised Jesus our Lord from the dead. "*

"Redemption" is a financial metaphor. Remember Green Stamps® ? Remember going to the Green Stamp redemption center where you could "redeem" your stamps for lovely toasters, etc.? The truth was, you had paid for that toaster already (many times over!). But you still had to go and, in a sense, buy it back from the company. *"For he has rescued us from the dominion of darkness and brought us into the kingdom of the Son he loves, in whom we have redemption, the forgiveness of sins"* (*Colossians 1:13-14*).

"Atonement" (the Greek word ιλασμος is sometimes translated "propitiation") means that God's righteous wrath against sin has been satisfied. The New Testament tells us that Christians will experience "tribulation" (persecutions and trials by the world and the evil one) but never "wrath" (God's righteous purging and punishment of sin). *"He [Jesus] is the atoning sacrifice*

*for our sins, and not only for ours but also for the sins of the
whole world"* (*I John 2:2*).

Note once again the framers' emphasis on the fact that Christ
"truly" suffered, was truly crucified, was truly dead, and was
truly buried. Again, this is not metaphorical language but a de-
scription and affirmation of real history.

> **III. Of the going down of Christ into Hell.** As Christ died for us,
> and was buried; so also is it to be believed, that he went down
> into Hell.

There is a good bit of controversy about what the concept of
Christ's descent "into Hell" means. The references to this in Scripture (*Psalm 16:10, Acts 2:27, 31, and I Peter 3:18-20*) are rather
ambiguous. At the time of Jesus, the concept of life after death
was a contentious one. Paul used this division of opinion to great
effect in one of his trials (see *Acts 23*).

The concept of any "punishment," let alone Hell, is unpleas-
ant to our culture. Our prisons are not called "penitentiaries"
(places of penance for sins) but "correctional institutions" (where
people who were, somehow, incorrect are now "corrected"). The
concept that there is a "badness" or an "unholiness" that needs
"redemption" is very unpopular today. The doctrine of Hell is
tied inexorably to the doctrine of the holiness and justice of God.
In order for Jesus to pay the full price for sin, He needed to drink
from the dregs of God's righteous wrath.

It is helpful in this regard to compare the death of Jesus to
the death of Socrates. Socrates (who died about 400 years before Christ's birth) drank the hemlock with calm resignation.
For him death was natural, even an adventure. Contrast that
with Jesus in the Garden. Jesus knew that death was unnatu-
ral, a corruption of His Father's original intent for the world.
And He knew that Hell was the punishment for sin, neither
some vague state of non-existence nor a light-filled journey
to a new state of consciousness.

American theologian H. Richard Neibuhr once described the
tendency to avoid the harsh doctrines of The Faith this way: "A
God without wrath brought a people without sin into a kingdom without judgement through the ministrations of a Christ

without a cross." Among many others, this article is a tonic against those merciful but mushy-headed tendencies.

> **IV. Of the Resurrection of Christ.** Christ did truly rise again from death, and took again his body, with flesh, bones, and all things appertaining to the perfection of Man's nature; wherewith he ascended into Heaven, and there sitteth, until he return to judge all Men at the last day.

This article unashamedly affirms that Christ did *truly* rise again and that His risen body had flesh, bones, and "all things appertaining to the perfection of Man's nature." In other words, not only was He not an apparition, He was a perfect human specimen.

Rabbis were not known for tight, syllogistic reasoning. But in his letter to the Christians at Corinth, Paul lays out a compelling case for the necessity of the bodily resurrection for the forgiveness of sins.

> *But if it is preached that Christ has been raised from the dead, how can some of you say that there is no resurrection of the dead? If there is no resurrection of the dead, then not even Christ has been raised. And if Christ has not been raised, our preaching is useless and so is your faith. More than that, we are then found to be false witnesses about God, for we have testified about God that he raised Christ from the dead. But he did not raise him if in fact the dead are not raised. For if the dead are not raised, then Christ has not been raised either. And if Christ has not been raised, your faith is futile; you are still in your sins. Then those also who have fallen asleep in Christ are lost. If only for this life we have hope in Christ, we are to be pitied more than all men* (I Corinthians 15:12-19).

Let us not kid ourselves. It is not noble and enlightened to contend for a Christianity that is devoid of a bodily resurrection. According to Paul, those who do so are not to be admired for their intellectual daring; they are to be pitied.

Finally, we must point out that, if we dispense with the bodily resurrection of Jesus as some sort of first century mythology or misplaced piety, we automatically forfeit not only His ascension but also the hope of His return. If He did not rise from the dead, then He could not have ascended and, if He did not ascend, He cannot come again in glory. And if He cannot come again to bring history to a close and to judge the living and dead, then the universe really is a brutish place with no hope of justice. To quote Shakespeare, it is "a tale told by an idiot, full of sound and fury, signifying nothing."

> **V. Of the Holy Ghost.** The Holy Ghost, proceeding from the Father and the Son, is of one substance, majesty, and glory, with the Father and the Son, very and eternal God.

This is the last of the articles on the Godhead. It seems that the Holy Spirit is often last when it comes to statements of Faith. The fact that it was included at all represents something of a modification of the earlier documents for there was nothing corresponding to this Article in the Forty-two Articles of 1553, and there was none in the confession of Augsburg. It was derived entirely from the Confession of Württemburg, presented to the Council of Trent, 1552, and introduced in England in 1563. The purpose was probably simply to give greater completeness to the presentation of Christian doctrine. There does, however, seem to have been a reason why it was included beyond a simple desire to be comprehensive.[109] Just like today, while the Church of the 16th century had its "formalists," it also had its enthusiasts.[110] There were those who believed that the Holy Spirit was all one needed to live the Christian life, that He indwelt the heart and informed the mind of the believer, and that the inner promptings of the Spirit were self-justifying. On the other hand there were those who felt that the essential truth of the Christian faith was found in the traditions and liturgies of the Church and in the text of sacred Scripture. The Anglican Church has historically been prone to fall off on only one side of that horse — the "formalist" side. Yet, a balance, however hard to achieve, is the only way to get along and stay *on* the horse.

The article makes no mention of the role of the Holy Spirit, only of His character. It affirms the Nicean formulation that the

---

109   Thomas, p. 90.

110   Literally "those in god" (*en-theos*), implying in that age an ecstatic union with visible and unusual manifestations.

Holy Spirit is a co-equal member of the Godhead with all that this entails.

The attentive reader will note that this article assumes and affirms the hotly debated and now optional *filioque* (Latin for *and the Son*) clause. This clause in the Nicene Creed affirmed that the Spirit proceeded from the Father *and* the Son. Its inclusion in the western version of the Creed since around the year 1,000 has been a stumbling block for reunion with many Eastern and Orthodox churches which have always maintained that the Spirit proceeds only from the Father. Its inclusion in the Nicene Creed became optional in the Episcopal Church in America in 1994.

This rather arcane sounding discussion does raise the question of the role of the Holy Spirit in creative and redemptive history. To do even passing justice to the subject would take a volume much larger than this one. Many excellent books have been written on the subject. What is important in this context, though, is to note that the Anglican Church has always affirmed the majesty and ministry of the Holy Spirit in the life of The Church and in the lives of its members — since its members are, first and foremost, members of the Body of Christ.

> **VI. Of the Sufficiency of the Holy Scriptures for Salvation.** Holy Scripture containeth all things necessary to salvation: so that whatsoever is not read therein, nor may be proved thereby, is not to be required of any man, that it should be believed as an article of the Faith, or be thought requisite or necessary to salvation. In the name of the Holy Scripture we do understand those canonical Books of the Old and New Testament, of whose authority was never any doubt in the Church.

> **Of the Names and Number of the Canonical Books.** Genesis, The First Book of Samuel, The Book of Esther, Exodus, The Second Book of Samuel, The Book of Job, Leviticus, The First Book of Kings, The Psalms, Numbers, The Second Book of Kings, The Proverbs, Deuteronomy, The First Book of Chronicles, Ecclesiastes or Preacher, Joshua, The Second Book of Chronicles, Cantica, or Songs of Solomon, Judges, The First Book of Esdras, Four Prophets the greater, Ruth, The Second Book of Esdras, Twelve Prophets the less.

And the other Books (as Hierome saith) the Church doth read for example of life and instruction of manners; but yet doth it not apply them to establish any doctrine; such are these following: The Third Book of Esdras, The rest of the Book of Esther, The Fourth Book of Esdras, The Book of Wisdom, The Book of Tobias, Jesus the Son of Sirach, The Book of Judith, Baruch the Prophet, The Song of the Three Children, The Prayer of Manasses, The Story of Susanna, The First Book of Maccabees, Of Bel and the Dragon, The Second Book of Maccabees.

All the Books of the New Testament, as they are commonly received, we do receive, and account them Canonical.

The next two articles (VI & VII) have to do with the nature of Holy Scripture. It has been noted that, in a purely logical and syllogistic sense, these articles are out of order. Since we may only gain authoritative truth about God from the pages of Scripture, it seems only logical that the article which affirms the veracity and reliability of Scripture should be the first statement. Many of the other 16th century confessions put affirmations about Scripture as their first declaration. This subtle distinction is one of the things that separates Anglicans from some of the more stridently biblio-centric communions. As was noted above, the framers of the Articles chose to follow the example of Paul on the *Aeropagus* in their apologetic, arguing first for the nature of God and only then introducing as a discreet topic the nature of God's Word.

It is also important, and equally subtle in its presentation, that the Articles on Scripture precede the Articles on the nature of the Church. The Church derives its authority from Scripture (see Articles XIX & XX) not *vice versa*. Just as the Church does not make Jesus Lord by receiving Him as Lord, neither does the Church make Scripture the Word of God, it only receives it as such.[111] Jesus is Lord whether anyone acknowledges the fact or not. Scripture is the Word of God whether anyone acknowledges the fact or not.

---

111 The language chosen by the Council of Trent also made this same point when it said the Church "receives and venerates . . . . all the books of the Old and New Testament. . . . "

The original intent of this article was clearly to refute the medieval Roman Catholic doctrine that knowledge of salvation was found partly in the Scriptures but also partly in the infallible teachings of the Church. And not just as the Church interpreted the text of Scripture, but as the Church added to the Scriptures those things that God laid upon its collective consciousness. This article refutes that notion, but it goes even farther.

We have discussed the Anglican tenet of *Lex Orandi—Lex Credendi* — the law of praying is the law of believing. In other words, one way to learn what Anglicans believe is to listen to them pray. In that light, examine carefully this prayer from *The Book of Common Prayer:*

> *Blessed Lord, who caused all holy Scriptures to be written for our learning: Grant us so to hear them, read, mark, learn, and inwardly digest them, that we may embrace and ever hold fast the blessed hope of everlasting life, which you have given us in our Savior Jesus Christ; who lives and reigns with you and the Holy Spirit, one God, for ever and ever.*

The prayer starts with a bold affirmation — that it was God Himself Who caused all holy Scriptures (not just a few selected verses here or there) to be written for our learning. The petition is that we, as His people, would literally consume them and that they would become a part of us. Does that notion sound strange? It is no less than what Jesus meant when He said to his disciples, *"It is written: 'Man does not live on bread alone, but on every word that comes from the mouth of God'"* (Matthew 4:4).

The initial affirmation in this article, that the Scriptures contain all things necessary to salvation, is a restatement of Paul's advice to Timothy. *"But as for you, continue in what you have learned and have become convinced of, because you know those from whom you learned it, and how from infancy you have known the holy Scriptures, which are able to make you wise for salvation through faith in Christ Jesus. All Scripture is God-breathed and is useful for teaching, rebuking, correcting and training in righteousness, so that the man of God may be thoroughly equipped for every good work"* (II Timothy 3:14-17).

The Articles wisely do not claim that the Scriptures contain all knowledge, only that they contain "all things necessary to salvation." What can this mean?

The first thing many western Anglicans often have to get beyond is a rather unfortunate, visceral reaction to the word "salvation." I once overheard one visitor at an Episcopal worship service ask another when the "altar call" came. The second responded that Episcopalians don't have "altar calls." After a thoughtful pause, the first then asked, "Well, how can you get saved in an Episcopal Church?" The second answered, "You can't."

At this point I couldn't help but interrupt, admit I had been eavesdropping, and try to set this sincere but misguided gentleman straight. I pointed out that Episcopalians "get saved" the same way every other Christian gets saved, by appropriating personally what Christ did for them on the cross. And yes, Episcopalians do indeed have "altar calls" every Sunday. We call it Holy Communion. Some Episcopal churches (including the one I serve) also have times when people are invited to come forward and pray to receive Christ as their Lord and Savior — to "get saved."

I have much more to say on this but you cannot bear it now. (See also the discussion on Articles IX, X, XI, & XVII.)

It may seem odd to the reader, but the question, "How can one get saved?" is deceptively prevalent in our society. Deceptive because it is rarely phrased just that way in our culture. We are more likely to hear someone say something like, "My life is so empty, what does it all mean?" or "I've got this personal problem I just can't lick. Can you help me?" etc. What the person is trying to say is, quite simply, "I am lost and need to be found. I am drowning and I need to be saved."

Perhaps the second thing many Anglicans need to get beyond is that anything is necessary to salvation at all — other than death, of course. Our culture has largely resolved the Reformation argument justification by faith vs. justification by works with the simple formula: justification by death. This, of course, is simply "universalism" and will be discussed more under Article XVIII.

The notion that something other than simply dying is necessary to being "saved" comes as a shock to most people and a shocking number of Christian people. But, the Scripture is not only the repository of all things necessary to salvation, it makes it clear that God does require faith in His Son Jesus Christ in order to be saved. As the Philippian jailor asked Paul and Silas: ". . . *'Sirs, what must I do to be saved?' They replied, 'Believe in the Lord Jesus, and you will be saved — you and your household' "(Acts 16:30-31)*.

Of course, if that is all there were to it, the Bible would be a very short book indeed. The gracious gift of salvation offered in Jesus Christ is the culmination of eons of what biblical scholars have dramatically dubbed *heilsgeshichte (salvation history)*. Even the apparently simple admonition to "believe" can become the subject of a mind-numbing number of nuances (see, for example, *James 2:19*).

The Scriptures are the story of God's constant, steadfast love toward His people, and His gracious offer of salvation, eternal life with Him to any who would simply respond to Him in faith. Within its pages are countless treasures that can evoke and enliven faith. The article itself hints at this when it speaks of doctrines that may be "read therein" or "proved thereby."

There are two basic methods of Bible study that any serious Christian should know. The first is often called "inductive study" and involves simply reading the text to see what it says. That is the "read therein" part of the article. The technical term for this method is *exegesis*, the art/science of getting out of the text what God placed in there. It's like exploring a new and fascinating country.

The second method, "deductive study," is the "proved thereby" part. It is more like mining for gold than exploring a new country. You know what you are looking for. You know the gold is there, you just have to find it. In this method the reader comes at the text with a notion already in mind. Then (when this method is used honestly) the task becomes to see if the text supports the notion. It is not unlike what a lawyer or a scientist does when he or she tests a case or a theory against the evidence.

Whatever method the disciple chooses, the important thing is to be spending time reading, marking, learning, and inwardly digesting the Scriptures because they are able to make the reader wise for salvation.

It must be pointed out that this article does contain a bit of hyperbole. When the article says that the "canon"[112] of Scripture contains only those books "of whose authority was never any doubt in the church," that is a stretch. While the canon of Scripture was virtually complete by the year 220 A.D., doubt persisted for some years about certain N. T. books such as James, Revelation and the Epistles of Peter. The issue of which books were properly received into the life of the church was officially ended by the fifth century.[113] The process has been summarized (and perhaps overly simplified) this way:[114]

A.D. 50-100: composing, writing

A.D. 100-200: collecting, gathering

A.D. 200-300: comparing, sifting

A.D. 300-400: completing, recognizing

Scholarly work continues to this day on exactly how some texts should read. (See, for example, the end of the *Gospel of Mark* and *John 7:53 - 8:11*.) But these issues do not affect the ultimate authority of the books in particular or the Bible as a whole.

It should be noted also that this article is the only place where the Anglican Church names which books it accepts as canonical. The Bible is referred to in other places in *The Book of Common Prayer*, and the Lectionary specifies certain pericopes (sections) of Scripture that are to be read on certain days, but nowhere else is there a list of the books of the Bible that the Anglican Church accepts as the Word of God written. If the Articles

---

112 The word "canon" is a Greek word that means "straight rod or bar" and, thus, it came to mean a "rule" or "guide" by which decisions are made — hence also the word "cane." It was first used within the Christian Church by a poet, Amphilochius, in 380 A.D. and was picked up by Jerome and Augustine (*ca* 400).

113   The first official, corporate witness to the whole canon comes from the Council of Laodicea in 364 A.D. (Thomas, p. 107).

114   Thomas, p. 111.

of Religion are completely removed from the life of this communion, no authority will exist that specifies what books constitute what the Episcopal Church means when it refers to "the Bible." Think about it.

By the way, less than a dozen citations from the Apocrypha appear in the entire three-year Lectionary of the Episcopal Church, and many of those are optional readings.

> **VII. Of the Old Testament.** The Old Testament is not contrary to the New: for both in the Old and New Testament everlasting life is offered to Mankind by Christ, who is the only Mediator between God and Man, being both God and Man. Wherefore they are not to be heard, which feign that the old Fathers did look only for transitory promises. Although the Law given from God by Moses, as touching Ceremonies and Rites, do not bind Christian men, nor the Civil precepts thereof ought of necessity to be received in any commonwealth; yet notwithstanding, no Christian man whatsoever is free from the obedience of the Commandments which are called Moral.

One of the earliest heresies to hit the Christian Church was the error of a fellow named Marcion. Marcion believed that, with the advent of Jesus and God's final and most perfect covenant, there was no longer any need to honor or even read the Old Testament. In fact, Marcion went so far to say that the Old Testament revealed a lesser god than the one revealed in the New Testament. In Marcion's view, the Old Testament God was petty, jealous, and mean. The God of the New Testament, the one whom Jesus came to reveal, was loving, kind and merciful.

Even though he was condemned as a heretic and died about 160 A.D., the notion that Christians don't really need the Old Testament is still alive and well. And, many Christians, even many clergy and bishops, hold to a subconscious, or subtle, form of this ancient heresy. This article affirms that the Old Testament is not contrary to the new and that it still has relevance for today.

The article makes a distinction between what have been called the "cultic"[115] laws of the Old Covenant, those that related specifically to "ceremonies and rites," and the moral law. The cultic regulations of the Old Testament (kosher food laws, for example) no longer apply to Christians. This question was first addressed and largely settled at the Council of Jerusalem (see *Acts 15*). The moral law, however, because it reflects the eternal character of God, is still binding on Christians. The Ten Commandments, for example, still hold moral authority for Christians. If anything, Jesus made the requirements imposed by the moral law even more stringent (see, for example, *Matthew 5*).

So, on the one hand, the article was addressed to a certain antinomian (the best law is no law) sentiment that was prevalent in the 16th century, especially among some of the radical Anabaptist groups. But there were other forces at work on the other end of the spectrum. These were the "Reconstructionists."

Any time a society experiences the sort of upheaval and turmoil that engulfed the 16th century, people look about for models of how to reorder society. One temptation among well-meaning Christians has always been to look to the Old Testament as a blueprint for not just a well-ordered society but a goodly and Godly society. "What better textbook on everything from crop rotation to civil government than the very words of God?" The problem, of course, is that while God's very specific instructions about how to order society worked quite well for a semi-nomadic people just coming out of 400 years of slavery in a country that worshiped its earthly king as a god and were about to enter into a land none of them had ever occupied, many of those same rules do not work nearly as well in 16th century Europe or in 21st century America.

Just as the 16th century reformers faced problems on the one hand from antinomian Marcionites and from reconstructionists on the other, so also the Church today faces similar problems.

There are well meaning Christian people who look at the Old Testament and say it is irrelevant in our modern world. This ten-

---

115   The word "cultic" here is used in its technical sense, not its colloquial sense. Its technical sense carries no sense of judgement and refers only to a system of religious practices. The more common, colloquial sense of the word implies that such practices are fanatical, abnormal, and/or idiosyncratic in the extreme.

dency is especially evident in discussions about sexuality. There are those who would argue that because Jesus never mentioned homosexuality the Church should not either. They ignore, of course, the fact that Jesus was a practicing Jew who would have assumed that the Old Testament prohibitions were still binding.

There are also well-meaning Christians who respond to the daunting challenges of life in 21st century America and Europe by advocating a return to the Old Testament societal structure. These "reconstructionists" range from thoughtful Bible scholars to fanatical (and ironically often anti-Semitic) para-military separatist groups. As this article states so clearly, both extremes are equally destructive to The Faith and to the very fabric of society.

One final note: The careful reader will have noticed that no comparable article on the New Testament is included. None was needed. The Great Reformation was a movement based solidly in the New Testament, and its authority was unquestioned and unequivocal.

> **VIII. Of the Creeds.** The Nicene Creed, and that which is commonly called the Apostles' Creed, ought thoroughly to be received and believed: for they may be proved by most certain warrants of Holy Scripture. (The original Article given Royal assent in 1571 and reaffirmed in 1662, was entitled "Of the Three Creeds; and began as follows, "The Three Creeds, Nicene Creed, Athanasius's Creed, and that which is commonly called the Apostles' Creed ...")

The two creeds named in this article (Nicene and Apostles') will be familiar to anyone who has spent any time in an Anglican Church. The Nicene Creed is used in the communion service and the Apostles' Creed is used in The Daily Office and at baptisms and confirmations.

The origin of the Apostles' Creed is uncertain, but it is so clearly ancient and orthodox that it has come to be called the creed of the Apostles even though it is almost certain that none of the first apostles had anything to do with the actual framing of it.

The Nicene Creed grew out of the ecumenical Council of Nicea (*ca* 325 A.D.). The version used in most editions of *The Book of Common Prayer* is an expanded version of the original creed. The key issue at debate in Nicea, and the *raison d'être* for the creed, was the nature of the incarnation. Was Jesus Christ fully God and/or fully human and/or some*thing* or *someone* else altogether? The Nicean formulary, that Jesus was of "one substance" with the Father, carried the day.

This deceptively complex doctrine is given fuller expression in the other creed mentioned in the original text of the article — the Creed of St. Athanasius. This magnificent but cumbersome statement of orthodox Christology is found, along with the Chalcedonian Creed, in the *Historical Documents* section of the *BCP*, p. 864. If you plan to study these precise but ponderous statements (as I hope and pray you will) plan to pack a lunch, take two aspirin, and remember what C. S. Lewis said about the true Truth being complex.

Perhaps the most important point this article makes is that the creeds are acceptable because they may be proved by Scripture, not *vice versa*. Once again, we see that the Scriptures are the ultimate guide and canon for The Faith.

> **IX. Of Original or Birth-Sin.** Original sin standeth not in the following of Adam, (as the Pelagians do vainly talk;) but it is the fault and corruption of the Nature of every man, that naturally is engendered of the offspring of Adam; whereby man is very far gone from original righteousness, and is of his own nature inclined to evil, so that the flesh lusteth always contrary to the Spirit; and therefore in every person born into this world, it deserveth God's wrath and damnation. And this infection of nature doth remain, yea in them that are regenerated; whereby the lust of the flesh, called in Greek, φρόνημα σαρκός, (which some do expound the wisdom, some sensuality, some the affection, some the desire, of the flesh), is not subject to the Law of God. And although there is no condemnation for them that believe and are baptized; yet the Apostle doth confess, that concupiscence and lust hath of itself the nature of sin.

Very few observers of the human condition would maintain that humankind is not, in some sense, "fallen." While they may not use that term, there is a conviction that something, somewhere, somehow has caused humanity to reflect a perplexing paradox. Humans are capable of glorious achievement and nobility and, at the same time, hideous acts of cruelty and debauchery that border on the diabolical. How do civilized, intelligent people account for the fact that civilization is so often uncivilized?

The Christian's answer is that since The Garden, humankind has been tainted by "original sin." Having said that, we must admit that this doctrine is a tough sell today. It flies in the face of much of what we were taught about the nature of humankind from grade-school on up. Notions of the essential goodness and perfectability of the autonomous self permeate our culture from Hallmark cards to debates about welfare reform to the loftiest ivory towers of academia.

Perhaps no other Christian doctrine so separates orthodox Christians from the prevailing, "enlightened" views of their contemporaries. No other dogma so rankles the ranks of unbelieving men and women as does the assertion that they are "inclined to evil," "a sinner from their mother's womb" (*Psalm 51*), and "deserving of God's wrath and damnation." Is it faithfulness or folly to maintain such a theology in this day and age?

The Pelagians were distant followers of a fifth century cleric named Pelagius who was condemned by Augustine. Pelagianism is "the heresy which holds that man can take the initial and fundamental steps towards salvation by his own efforts."[116] Implicit in this assertion is the assumption that each person is born in a state of sinless innocence and that sin enters the life of each person as that individual person sins. The Pelagians basically believed that as soon as a person could sin, he or she would sin, so the practical effect of the distinction on the "real" world was nil. But the implications for a systematic understanding of God's saving work in Christ were significant.

The Pelagians wanted to do away with the whole concept of "imputed guilt," that, in the words of the old primer, "In Adam's fall, we sinned all." This view has also been called "Federal theology" because it views Adam as the true representative of the

---

116 *Oxford Dictionary of the Christian Church*, p. 1058.

human race for all time. Paul seems to allude to this understanding in *I Corinthians 15:22 & 45*. Herein lies the crux of the issue.

If we do away with the concept of imputed guilt from Adam's fall, we also, by implication, do away with the imputed righteousness of Christ's atonement. There's a sense in which we can't have it both ways. We cannot say in one breath that it is not fair for God to condemn us for what Adam did so long ago and far away (especially when so few people believe in Adam as an historical person anymore anyway) and still ask God to forgive us on the basis of what Christ did so long ago and far away (especially when so few clerics believe that Jesus did what the Bible says He did anyway).

In his classic *Mere Christianity*, C. S. Lewis uses the analogy of a good *vs* a bad infection. We were born with a "bad" infection, one that draws us away from God and toward death. In his grace, God imputes (injects?) us with a "good" infection — His Holy Spirit — that draws us towards Him and into life. This analogy is helpful because it fits with the other key point that the article makes, that our justification (being declared righteous in God's sight) does not mean our earthly perfection. We still retain our "carnal" (fleshly) nature and we still will sin. (See Articles XI, XII, XV, & XVI.) This is what the Apostle Paul was wrestling with in his famous passage to the Christians at Rome.

Before he came to know Christ, Paul was the picture of self-confidence and righteous pride (see *Philippians 3:4-6*). But after being confronted with the perfection of Christ, his attitude changed and he became aware of just how pervasive and deadly his own sinful nature was (see *Romans 7:21-25*). The new life in Christ promises strength and forgiveness, but not perfection in this life.

Now, if you think this doctrine was controversial, wait till you read the next one.

> **X. Of Free-Will.** The condition of Man after the fall of Adam is such, that he cannot turn and prepare himself, by his own natural strength and good works, to faith; and calling upon God. Wherefore we have no power to do good works pleasant and acceptable to God, without the grace of God by Christ prevent-

ing us, that we may have a good will, and working with us, when we have that good will.

This article naturally and systematically follows the one before, but it really rubs a raw nerve, especially in a culture for which the rugged individual is the ideal. Unfortunately, sin has corrupted this superficially noble ideal of the self-made man by replacing it with the man-made self.

Comedian and singer Noel Stookey has observed that in one generation our culture has turned ever inward, the trend reflected in a progression of magazine titles from *Life* to *People* (a small part of life), to *Us* (a small part of people), to *Self* (a very small part of us).

This article states quite simply and bluntly that, after the fall, human beings are incapable of turning toward God unless God Himself "helps" us. (Ironically, this is the old meaning of the word "preventing." It comes from the Latin meaning "to come" and, with the prefix, *pre-* it means "to come before," or to assist. Isn't it odd how language develops!?)

After the fall, human wills are bound by the "sinful desires that draw (us) from the love of God" (*BCP* p. 302). This insight is what caused Martin Luther to write his classic apologetic for the Protestant understanding of the Gospel, *The Bondage of the Will*. It was his rediscovery of this doctrine that can be clearly traced through Augustine back to Paul that helped him to realize he could not get to heaven by trying harder. God had to change our wills to conform to His will. God had to release us from our will from bondage — and only God could do that because, in our sinful state, we were *"dead in sin and tresspasses"* (*Ephesians 2:1-5*).

We'll say more about this in Article XVII.

> **XI. Of the Justification of Man.** We are accounted righteous before God, only for the merit of our Lord and Savior Jesus Christ by Faith, and not for our own works or deservings. Wherefore, that we are justified by Faith only, is a most wholesome Doctrine, and very full of comfort, as more largely is expressed in the Homily of Justification.

My mother always said I should have been an accountant. It pleases me on a very existential level when things line up and the books balance.

There are few things more satisfying than paying off a huge debt. The day when a church, or a person, burns the mortgage rivals Easter as a day of celebration and release. Yet, what can we do when the debt is too great to pay, when there is no way the ledger can be reconciled, when no amount of accounting finesse can balance the books?

Before the atonement of Christ, and the redemption and reconciliation He has made available, this was our condition before a holy and righteous God. Our debt was eternal and the penalty was death. But Christ paid the debt. His merit, His righteousness, was "credited" to our account. Thus, we are "accounted" righteous before God. We are not made righteous spiritually, we are declared righteous legally. It is what theologians call forensic righteousness. This was the burden of Paul's argument in *Romans 4* as he makes a case for God's declarative gift of righteousness for Abraham on the basis of faith, not works. *"Abraham believed the Lord and it was credited to him as righteousness" (Romans 4:3).*

One of the banners of the Reformation was *Sola Fide, Sola Gratia — By Faith alone, By Grace alone* are we saved. Think of grace as a boulder floating upstream, as a snow-day when you had not prepared for a test, as "God's Riches At Christ's Expense."

Remember the computer keys (or mouse clicks) that indicate "justification" and "reconciliation"? In Christ, by grace through faith, the believer is justified (brought into alignment with God's justice) and reconciled (debts paid and books balanced).

> **XII. Of Good Works.** Albeit that Good Works, which are the fruits of Faith, and follow after Justification, cannot put away our sins, and endure the severity of God's judgment; yet are they pleasing and acceptable to God in Christ, and do spring out necessarily of a true and lively Faith; insomuch that by them a lively Faith may be as evidently known as a tree discerned by the fruit.

We had a resolution once at a convention to the effect that we ought to pray. Even though virtually everyone thought the resolution was so benign as to be superfluous, no one in their right mind was going to say so publicly. How can one speak against prayer at a church convention? So, there it was. It passed. We prayed.

This article is a little like that resolution. It states that good works are, well, good. Jesus (*Matthew 7:16-20*), John the Baptist (*Matthew 3:10*), and Paul (*Galatians 5:22, 23*) had all made the point that fruit, figuratively speaking, was the evidence of a lively faith. In the world of horticulture, fruit is the result of health and maturity. It is the same in the spiritual world. Just as unhealthy or immature plants produce inadequate fruit, so also do unhealthy or immature Christians.

And, just as apple trees do not live on apples, so also Christians do not live off their own fruit. Christians bear fruit for others' nourishment and strengthening.

A "good work," by definition, is the fruit of faith, not of an arbitrary or self-serving motive. Which leads us to the next article.

> **XIII. Of Works before Justification.** Works done before the grace of Christ, and the Inspiration of his Spirit, are not pleasant to God, forasmuch as they spring not of faith in Jesus Christ; neither do they make men meet to receive grace, or (as the School-authors say) deserve grace of congruity: yea rather, for that they are not done as God hath willed and commanded them to be done, we doubt not but they have the nature of sin.

The burden of this article was to demonstrate that works done outside of a relationship with God, even if they are apparently "good" works, cannot please God. This is counter-intuitive to most people in our culture, even to most Christians. How is it possible that so many "good" people who do so many "good" things are not pleasing God when they do them? And why don't they get any credit for the "good" things they have done? Doesn't God care? Would He just as soon people acted "badly"?

Of course not. Yes, God does care. And He does apportion common grace to the world so that His creation will not be destroyed by unrestrained wickedness. But the whole concept of what constitutes a "good" action can be very tricky, unless, like God, we can see the heart. Let me illustrate, but first, remember that it was the ungodly and rebellious desire to know good and evil that led to humankind's expulsion from The Garden.

Imagine, if you will, a modern super-highway with a posted speed limit of 65 mph. Everyone is tooling along at 75 mph trusting in luck and the largess of the local constabulary. But, the long arm of absolute justice has decided to enforce the law to the letter and everyone gets pulled over — everyone that is except Dudley Goodriver who is driving exactly 65 mph. They pull him over and give him a good citizenship medal and a citation suitable for framing. He was the only one obeying the law that day.

What they did not see was Dudley when he turned off the highway onto a back country road. There the speed limit was 35 mph but he still drove 65 mph. It turns out he drives 65 mph because he likes to drive 65 mph. He drives that speed no matter what the law is. When he is in a 65 mph zone, he is an apparent paragon of virtue and self-control. When he isn't, he's a scofflaw.[117]

Of course the reality is that Dudley is a law unto himself. His apparent good deeds are nothing but selfishness that happens, on occasion, to appear as a righteousness born of virtue.

Let me give another, more Biblical example. When Jesus was tempted by the Evil One to turn stones into bread, there was nothing inherently evil about the action itself. In fact, if one could find a way to easily do that it would be one of the greatest boons to humankind in history. In other words, the temptation Jesus faced was not to do something intrinsically "bad," only to do something that His Father had not requested of Him.

A surprising number of actions are, in that sense, morally neutral. That is not to say their moral value is "relative." They only have moral value as they relate to some absolute, in this case, the perfect and pleasing will of God.

One final example should suffice: Two men are seen in the parking lot of a restaurant. One is spanking a small boy and the

---

117 The writer would like to credit Dr. R. C. Sproul for this illustration.

boy is crying. The other is giving another small boy a piece of candy and gently rubbing the boy's head. Which man is acting in a loving way?

Unless you knew that the man spanking the child was the child's father who was trying to instill an appreciation for justice into his child while the other man was a pedophile trying to lure a strange child into his car, it would be easy to misjudge which act was an act of righteousness and love. The motive behind the action, coupled with the intended result of the action, are what make a work "good" in the eyes of God.

"The Lord does not look at the things man looks at. Man looks at the outward appearance, but the Lord looks at the heart" (*1 Samuel 16:7*).

How can we determine if our actions are "good" in this sense? We begin by submitting them to the word of God: *"For the word of God is living and active. Sharper than any double-edged sword, it penetrates even to dividing soul and spirit, joints and marrow; it judges the thoughts and attitudes of the heart"* (*Hebrews 4:12*). We then see the advice and counsel of other believers whom we trust. Finally, we acknowledge, that in this life, we may never really know, for conscience itself — even an educated conscience — can be a deceptive guide. As the Apostle Paul said, *"I care very little if I am judged by you or by any human court; indeed, I do not even judge myself. My conscience is clear, but that does not make me innocent. It is the Lord who judges me. Therefore judge nothing before the appointed time; wait till the Lord comes"* (*I Corinthains 4:3-5*).

> **XIV. Of Works of Supererogation.** Voluntary Works besides, over and above, God's Commandments, which they call Works of Supererogation, cannot be taught without arrogancy and impiety: for by them men do declare, that they do not only render unto God as much as they are bound to do, but that they do more for his sake, than of bounden duty is required: whereas Christ saith plainly When ye have done all that are commanded to you, say, We are unprofitable servants.

No, "supererogation" does not have to do with some sort of fantastic sprinkler system. It is a very technical term meaning "works [*erg*] above and beyond those necessary for salvation." The Medieval Church taught that such works were possible and that such excess righteousness could be stored in a "Treasury of Merit." These "credits" could be drawn upon by lesser saints and sinners. Such accounts could be accessed by appealing to the great saints who had died with those credits "in the bank," so to speak.

This doctrine had led to the sale of "indulgences" in the Medieval Church and, as such, was the cause of much misery, poverty, and misunderstanding within the Church.

No one would argue that all people are the same in terms of apparent or purely human righteousness. By grace and disciplined obedience, some people do achieve laudable levels of piety, charity, and Christ-likeness. In our age, Mother Teresa provided a vivid example of what a person who is totally sold-out to Jesus can do. Yet, even Mother Teresa's righteousness could not be said to have *exceeded* the holiness and perfection God requires of His people.

The article ends by quoting Jesus (*Luke 17:10*) and His admonition that even perfect obedience is only the minimum expected of worthy servants. Ironically, it is the only direct quote from Jesus in the Articles.

> **XV. Of Christ alone without Sin**. Christ in the truth of our nature was made like unto us in all things, sin only except, from which he was clearly void, both in his flesh, and in his spirit. He came to be the Lamb without spot, who, by sacrifice of himself once made, should take away the sins of the world; and sin (as Saint John saith) was not in him. But all we the rest, although baptized and born again in Christ, yet offend in many things; and if we say we have no sin, we deceive ourselves, and the truth is not in us.

Articles X, XII-XIV state that humankind is incapable of producing a champion to carry our cause. We are incapable of bearing the load or paying the debt ourselves. It, therefore, follows naturally to ask, as Jesus' disciples did, "who then can be saved?" (*Mark 10:26*). Jesus' answer to that all-important question points us unwaveringly to His Cross. *"With man this is impossible, but not with God; all things are possible with God"* (*Mark 10:27*).

Again in *Mere Christianity*, C. S. Lewis writes about the "perfect penitent." The conundrum is this: Forgiveness requires repentance. The less perfect one is, the more one needs to repent but the less one is able to do it. The very badness that makes repentance necessary renders it impossible. Only a perfect person could repent perfectly, but he would not need to.

Only Jesus qualifies. Jesus, the only man without sin, in the words of the late Chaplain of the Senate, the Rev. Richard Halverson's intriguing phrase, was the only "normal" man Who ever lived. Thus, the only sinless Man chose to become sin so that sinners might be saved. *"God made him who had no sin to be sin for us, so that in him we might become the righteousness of God"* (*II Corinthians 5:21*).

The article ends with a quote from *I John 1:8-9* which both confronts and comforts us with the truth that sin abides in us but that forgiveness is available in the sacrifice of the sinless One.

> **XVI. Of Sin after Baptism.** Not every deadly sin willingly committed after Baptism is sin against the Holy Ghost, and unpardonable. Wherefore the grant of repentance is not to be denied to such as fall into sin after Baptism. After we have received the Holy Ghost, we may depart from grace given, and fall into sin, and by the grace of God we may arise again, and amend our lives. And therefore they are to be condemned, which say, they can no more sin as long as they live here, or deny the place of forgiveness to such as truly repent.

When I was younger and more self-assured, I suddenly found myself agonizing over a sin I had long ago committed (I had cheated on a test). My conscience would give me no peace until I went to the professor and confessed. The professor surprised me by receiving my confession with equanimity and a benevolence for which I had dared not hope. Instead of sending my academic career careening down the tubes, he give me a three sentence sermon I have never forgotten.

"One of the greatest deceptions of life," he said, "is to think that if we can just fix this one last thing about ourselves we will be perfect. It ain't gonna happen. Go in peace."

There was a teaching abroad in the land in the 16th century that humans could reach perfection in this life. That same teaching can be found today in some charismatic and Wesleyan traditions. I wish it were true, but, as my professor said, "It ain't."

> **XVII. Of Predestination and Election.** Predestination to Life is the everlasting purpose of God, whereby (before the foundations of the world were laid) he hath constantly decreed by his counsel secret to us, to deliver from curse and damnation those whom he hath chosen in Christ out of mankind, and to bring them by Christ to everlasting salvation, as vessels made to honour. Wherefore, they which be endued with so excellent a benefit of God, be called according to God's purpose by his Spirit working in due season: they through Grace obey the calling: they be justified freely: they be made sons of God by adoption: they be made like the image of his only-begotten Son Jesus Christ: they walk religiously in good works, and at length, by God's mercy, they attain to everlasting felicity.
>
> As the godly consideration of Predestination, and our Election in Christ, is full of sweet, pleasant, and unspeakable comfort to godly persons, and such as feel in themselves the working of the Spirit of Christ, mortifying the works of the flesh, and their earthly members, and drawing up their mind to high and heavenly things, as well because it doth greatly establish and confirm their faith of eternal Salvation to be enjoyed through Christ as because it doth fervently kindle their love towards God: So, for curious and carnal persons, lacking the Spirit of Christ, to have continually before their eyes the sentence of God's Predestination, is a most dangerous downfall, whereby the Devil doth thrust them either into desperation, or into wretchlessness of most unclean living, no less perilous than desperation.
>
> Furthermore, we must receive God's promises in such wise, as they be generally set forth to us in Holy Scripture: and, in our doings, that Will of God is to be followed, which we have expressly declared unto us in the Word of God.

I once went on a two-week wilderness adventure program called *Young Life's La Vida*. I knew the whole thing would be tough. Toward the end was a 12 mile marathon that involved scrambling over rocks, climbing mountains, canoeing from island to island, and generally getting beat up. I spent the whole trip dreading it. But then, when it finally came, I found the experience not only challenging but exhilarating. I was a better man for having worked through it, precisely because it was tough.

For many people, Article XVII is that marathon. They know it's coming and they dread dealing with it because they think it will beat them up — and for no good purpose. But, I think you will find that the work is worth the reward.

Using a very polite Anglican metaphor, that wonderfully bold Anglican John Newton, said, "Calvinism should be, in our general religious instructions, like a lump of sugar in a cup of tea; all should taste of it, but it should not be met with in a separate form."[118] "Calvinism" is one of those words that produces more heat than light and one of few words that provokes more Anglican angst than "saved."

Therefore, let's begin with some definitions and disclaimers. First, make it your goal to understand the teaching of this article before you decide whether or not you believe it. In that same light, earnestly pray that, in the words of the article itself, your "consideration" of this doctrine would be "godly."

Second, "Calvinism" has been used and abused over the centuries to describe a breathtaking variety of theological teachings. No one, least of all John Calvin, could possibly subscribe to each of its various contradictory manifestations. The "Calvinism" manifested in the Articles is of the kinder, gentler strain. As was discussed above, the more rigorous "Calvinism" of the Westminster divines and the Synod of Dort was rejected at the Hampton Court Conference in 1604.

But, lest the reader think that Anglicans thereby rejected the essential teaching of "Calvinism" (that God is intimately and actively involved from all eternity in bringing His people into a relationship with Himself), Article XVII pleads to be heard.

---

118 Bebbington, p. 63.

John Calvin
1509 — 1564

Third, some form of this doctrine has been an integral part of the vast majority of Christian dogma since there was such a thing as Christianity. Of course, Calvinists, fully aware of the amusing anachronism of the claim, claim that the Apostle Paul was a Calvinist (or, more properly, that Calvin had rightly discerned and described Paul's theology). The fact is that "Calvinism" was not an invention of the 16th century Reformation. Theologians from Augustine to Aquinas believed it and taught it.

Fourth, it is clearly impossible to do justice to this article in this brief context. We will, therefore, have to content ourselves with an inadequate, but hopefully accurate, rendering of the doctrine.

Fifth, we shall use the words "predestination" and "election" virtually synonymously. The word "elect," or some variation thereof, appears fourteen times in the New Testament. It is used by Jesus (*Matthew 24:22-24 and others*), and by Paul and Peter (*II Peter 1:10*). The word "predestined" appears only four times, each time from the pen of Paul. The Greek word translated "elect" ("elect" is actually its cognate) means to "select" or "choose." (If you don't like the word "election," try "selection.") The Greek word translated "predestined" is the word from which we get the word "horizon" and it means "to limit," the horizon being the limit of our vision.

Finally, please note that this article makes the startling claim that the doctrine is "full of sweet, pleasant, and unspeakable comfort to godly persons." Bear with us and we will show you how this works.

At the last supper, Jesus looked at his disciples and said, "*You did not choose me, but I chose you*[119] *and appointed you to go and bear fruit — fruit that will last*" (*John 15:16*). On one level, that is patently obvious. Jesus had walked along the Sea of Galilee and called certain people to be his disciples. He didn't just hang out a clipboard on a tree and ask for volunteers. But there is more going on here than that.

---

119 The word here translated "chose" in Greek is the same word translated elsewhere as "elect."

Throughout Scripture, there is a pattern of God's proactive and aggressive selection of people who, when you hear their stories, were not out looking for Him. Moses and David were tending sheep, Samuel was asleep in a corner, Jonah wanted to run away, Paul was on his way to kill Christians, etc.

God chose to reveal Himself in a saving way to Moses, not Pharaoh. God chose to work through the line of Jacob, not Esau. *"Yet, before the twins were born or had done anything good or bad — in order that God's purpose in election might stand: not by works but by him who calls — she was told, 'The older will serve the younger.' Just as it is written: 'Jacob I loved, but Esau I hated'* (Romans 9:11-13).

This seems unjust to us, or at least unfair. Well, it is unfair, but it is not unjust. Our society has confused justice with equality. Every parent knows that life is not fair but that's okay. God created each child as an individual and what may serve justice for one may not serve justice for another.

This question and concern did not catch Paul off guard. In the very next verses he says, *"What then shall we say? Is God unjust? Not at all! For he says to Moses, 'I will have mercy on whom I have mercy, and I will have compassion on whom I have compassion'"* (Romans 9:14-15).

Is there anything we can do about God's eternal decrees? Well, no. *"It does not, therefore, depend on man's desire or effort, but on God's mercy. For the Scripture says to Pharaoh: 'I raised you up for this very purpose, that I might display my power in you and that my name might be proclaimed in all the earth.' Therefore God has mercy on whom he wants to have mercy, and he hardens whom he wants to harden"* (Romans 9:16-18).

All this is complicated and seemingly harsh. Let me try to reduce it to three critical issues: ownership, justice and mercy. If we can get a handle on these, the rest will fall into place.

The first issue is ownership: *"Know ye that the Lord he is God: it is he that hath made us, and not we ourselves; we are his people, and the sheep of his pasture"* (Psalm 100:3 KJV). We must come to grips with the fact that God is our maker. He created us out of nothing. We are His, lock, stock, and barrel. He can do with us as He sees fit.

One of you will say to me: "Then why does God still blame us? For who resists his will?" But who are you, O man, to talk back to God? "Shall what is formed say to him who formed it, 'Why did you make me like this?' " Does not the potter have the right to make out of the same lump of clay some pottery for noble purposes and some for common use? (Romans 9:19-21)

He could have destroyed all of humankind in the days of Noah, but He chose to save a remnant to be His people. He could have done the same in the days of Sodom, and any time since then He chose. But His purpose was to redeem His people and adopt them into His family.

"For those God foreknew he also predestined to be conformed to the likeness of his Son, that he might be the firstborn among many brothers. And those he predestined, he also called; those he called, he also justified; those he justified, he also glorified" (Romans 8:29-30).

God did not do this to be mean! God did this to be merciful! His intention was to rescue us from death and adopt us as His children. *"He predestined us to be adopted as his sons through Jesus Christ, in accordance with his pleasure and will"* (Ephesians 1:5). All this is an extension of His ownership of us, and His ownership is not onerous.

The second critical issue with which we must deal is that of justice. We have already said that justice does not necessarily equate with equality. Can we have an example? Certainly, and watch carefully for how mercy enters the picture along with justice.

A teacher gave a test and collected the papers. Before she looked at them she said, "I am going to give everyone on the left side of the room 'A's' on this test. I am going to give everyone on the right side of the room whatever grade they deserve based on their performance on the test."

Was anyone in the class treated unjustly? No. The group on the right side got justice. They got what they deserved. The group on the left side got mercy, they got more than they deserved. But no one was treated unjustly.

And this brings us to the third critical element: mercy. If one would argue that if anyone receives mercy, then all must receive mercy, mercy is no longer mercy, it is justice. Mercy, by definition, cannot be mandated or coerced. God's mercy transcends His justice. It also transcends our understanding.

This distinction is vital to our understanding because of what was established earlier in Articles IX-XIII. What we deserve in our natural, sinful state, is death. For us to receive such an outcome IS justice. The fact that God chooses to save anyone from that outcome is all mercy and grace.

One final illustration. I was a chaplain in a shock-trauma unit in Washington, D.C. This large hospital had a separate "emergency room" for twisted ankles and small cuts, etc. The shock-trauma unit was only for life-threatening situations.

One night a young woman was hurried into the unit. She had been shot several times at close range. It turned out she was a prostitute, and she had been shot while she was "at work."

She had no pulse. For all intents and purposes, she was dead. The doctors and nurses worked feverishly and skillfully. The lead doctor took a scalpel and opened up her chest. He reached in and with his hands massaged her heart. She came back to life before my eyes. Afterwards, the other doctors and nurses patted him on the back and said something I would never forget: "Good save, Doc."

Good "save," indeed! What if, as the woman lay there with no heart beat, instead of the radical intervention by those medical doctors, the staff had looked at me as the chaplain and said, "Hey, Chaplain. This woman has been making some pretty poor choices about her life. Why don't you talk to her and get her to make better choices?"

I could have preached her a whale of a sermon about the wages of sin being death. But it was too late. She was already dead. She was incapable of responding to even the best sermon.

If she was to live again, someone would have to intervene. She needed to be brought back to life *before* she could make those good choices. That is what the doctors did for her. That is what God has done for us.

As for you, you were dead in your transgressions and sins, in which you used to live when you followed the ways of this world and of the ruler of the kingdom of the air, the spirit who is now at work in those who are disobedient. All of us also lived among them at one time, gratifying the cravings of our sinful nature and following its desires and thoughts. Like the rest, we were by nature objects of wrath. ***But*** *because of his great love for us,* ***God****, who is rich in mercy, made us alive with Christ even when we were dead in transgressions — it is by grace you have been saved"* (*Ephesians 2:1-5,* emphasis added).

Like that poor young woman, we were dead in sin. That was the penalty for sin way back in The Garden. Dead men make no choices. The Gospel can be summed up in those two little words *"But . . . God."* God is the One Who has chosen us. God is the One Who has saved us. Our salvation is secure because it is founded in His eternal purposes and His immutable character.

That is why this doctrine is "full of sweet, pleasant, and unspeakable comfort." As I said above, make sure you understand it before you decide to reject it. You could be missing something sweet.

> **XVIII. Of obtaining eternal Salvation only by the Name of Christ.**
> They also are to be had accursed that presume to say, That every man shall be saved by the Law or Sect which he professeth, so that he be diligent to frame his life according to that Law, and the light of Nature. For Holy Scripture doth set out unto us only the Name of Jesus Christ, whereby men must be saved.

This article articulates what has been called "the scandal of particularity." When Jesus said, *"I am the way, the truth and the life. No one comes to the Father but by me"* (*John 14:6*) did He mean that He was the only way to God? When the Apostle Peter said, *"Salvation is found in no one else, for there is no other name under heaven given to men by which we must be saved"* (*Acts 4:12*) did he mean that only in Jesus are we able to approach

God? When the Apostle Paul, quoting what appears to have been a contemporary hymn said, *"Therefore God exalted him to the highest place and gave him the name that is above every name, that at the name of Jesus every knee should bow, in heaven and on earth and under the earth, and every tongue confess that Jesus Christ is Lord, to the glory of God the Father,"* (Philippians 2:9-11) was he saying that Jesus is the one and only Lord of glory?

It seems so. This article clearly affirms that.

It also clearly affirms that Christian people are called upon to "frame (their lives) according to that Law and the light of Nature." To be a disciple implies, by definition, discipline. Too many Anglicans run in fear of being labeled "legalists" when what they want is simply to be obedient. A "legalist" is someone who thinks they can get to heaven by being good, or that God will love them more if they keep the rules. That is not true.

A devout and obedient Christian, on the other hand, is one who seeks consciously and conscientiously brings his or her life into conformity with that of Christ.

As someone once said, "For the Christian religion is grace and ethics is gratitude." Or, as Augustine said, "Love God and do as you please" because, if you truly love Him, it will please you to please Him.

> **XIX. Of the Church.** The visible Church of Christ is a congregation of faithful men, in which the pure Word of God is preached, and the Sacraments be duly ministered according to Christ's ordinance, in all those things that of necessity are requisite to the same. As the Church of Jerusalem, Alexandria, and Antioch, have erred, so also the Church of Rome hath erred, not only in their living and manner of Ceremonies, but also in matters of Faith.

This is the sort of sentence that makes one wish one had paid more time and attention to diagraming sentences. The two sentences in this article actually address two rather different thoughts. The first thought is to delineate what exactly constitutes a true church of God. This was a very pressing issue in the 16th century and, again in early 19th century America. It is a pressing issue again now. There are currently over 2,000 denominations in America with new ones being added all the time. Are all but one of them all wrong? Are all of them all right?

The second sentence in the article addresses an issue that may seem to be blatantly obvious to readers at the beginning of the third millennium after Christ; churches have erred in the past. But, this also was a pressing issue in the 16th century. To break with Rome meant, in the eyes of Rome and those who held to that allegiance, to break with an infallible church, the only infallible guide to faith and to the proper interpretation of the Bible.

It was clear that the reformers did not agree, and a fair reading of history will show that they were correct. The visible church, any visible church, is made up of sinful, fallible people. Even in the New Testament Paul had to rebuke Peter (for blatant hypocrisy — *Galatians 2:11-14*) and the Christians at Corinth (for licensing immorality — *I Corinthians 5:1-5*) and Jesus used the powerful pen of John the Beloved to rebuke several churches in his letter to the various churches in Revelation. Having noted and reaffirmed the obvious truth of the second sentence — and remembering to apply it to today's church as well, we can now return to the first sentence.[120]

According to this article, a true Church has three major attributes. First, it is "a congregation of faithful men (and women)." Anglicans are uneasy using the term "congregation" as synonymous with "church" for many of them believe the "diocese" to be the basic unit of the church. But, the Articles do not mention dioceses. The burden of the phrase, however, is not on polity but on faith. The primary attribute of the true Church is faithful people, for *"without faith it is impossible to please God"* (*Hebrews 11:6*).

But, both the 16th century and the late 20th were and are full of "faithful" people who believe all manner of nonsense. These

---

120 The sentence does raise one curious and rather entertaining quandary: If churches have erred, how can we know that the church was not in error when it broke from Rome or when it endorsed the Articles of Religion, etc.? It is what in philosophy is called *reductio ad absurdum*. It's like trying to prove the universe was not created 10 seconds ago precisely as we experience it now. It cannot be done. Once one has appealed to Scripture, Tradition, and Reason, all that's left is to take a walk and try to think about something more fruitful.

dear souls have "faith," but in all sorts of wrong things. They believe in tarot cards, horoscopes, crystals, pyramids, and that Elvis is still alive. Faith alone, without a fixed and worthy object, is no mark of a true church.

Thus, the article goes on to say that the true Church is one where the "pure Word of God is preached, and the Sacraments be duly administered." These two marks of the true Church conform to the symmetry of Christ's Great Commission to The Church: "*Go and make disciples of all nations, baptizing them in the name of the Father and of the Son and of the Holy Spirit, and teaching them to obey everything I have commanded you*" (*Matthew 28:19-20*).

The Great Commission has both a didactic/kerygmatic component and a sacramental component. The Church is not just a lecture hall where the people of God get good doctrine from the "pure Word of God," (although it is that) nor is it just a dispensary where the people of God come to have the Sacraments dispensed (although it is that as well). It must be both or it is neither.

The Anglican Church has historically held these two aspects of the Great Commission in balance better than most communions. It is easy for a church to fall into either a purely liturgical/sacramental routine that denies people solid expository preaching or into a routine that makes worship little more than a "hymn sandwich" where a long Bible study is bracketed by two hymns.

A church that is true to its high calling will honor both vocations.

> **XX. Of the Authority of the Church.** The Church hath power to decree Rites or Ceremonies, and authority in Controversies of Faith: and yet it is not lawful for the Church to ordain any thing that is contrary to God's Word written, neither may it so expound one place of Scripture, that it be repugnant to another. Wherefore, although the Church be a witness and a keeper of Holy Writ, yet, as it ought not to decree any thing against the same, so besides the same ought it not to enforce any thing to be believed for necessity of Salvation.

Queen Elizabeth was anxious to have the first clause in this article added. She was concerned about the growing popularity of informal gatherings of clergy and laity (called "prophesyings") that were spreading around England during the latter years of her reign and during the time of Archbishop of Canterbury, Edmund Grindal (d. 1583). These groups were really nothing more than collegial Bible studies, but Elizabeth wanted to make sure that the Church, of which she was the "supreme governor," had the final say in any controversy that might arise.

What is most significant, though, are not the powers which the articles retained to the Church, but those powers which it disclaimed. "It is not lawful for the Church to ordain any thing that is contrary to God's Word *written*." One wonders if many of the clerics and/or bishops of the Episcopal Church have read this article lately."God's word written" is the final test for any doctrine or dogma propounded by the Church.

Nor is the Church able to hide behind supposed ambiguities in the text for the Church may not "so expound one place of Scripture that it be repugnant to another." In other words, the Church is not free to say that Christians are free to ignore one part of Scripture because it is contradicted by another part. While it is legitimate to use the "rule of faith" (i.e., Scripture interprets Scripture) and to use a more clear passage of Scripture to illumine another that is less clear, it is not correct to set two passages in opposition to one another. Unfortunately, this is done far too often in far too many pulpits. This article is a caution against such an act.

The Church is the "witness and keeper of holy writ," neither creators nor redactors of it. Perhaps the Church so often fails to understand the text of Scripture because it first fails to stand under it.

> **XXI. Of the Authority of General Councils.** (The Twenty-first of the former Articles is omitted; because it is partly of a local and civil nature, and is provided for, as to the remaining parts of it, in other Articles.) (The original 1571, 1662 text of this Article, omitted in the version of 1801, reads as follows: "General Councils may not be gathered together without the commandment and will of Princes. And when they be gathered together, (forasmuch as they be an assembly of men, whereof all be not gov-

erned with the Spirit and Word of God,) they may err, and sometimes have erred, even in things pertaining unto God. Wherefore things ordained by them as necessary to salvation have neither strength nor authority, unless it may be declared that they be taken out of holy Scripture.")

This article is not overtly relevant in the American context where Church and state are largely separated. But, the attentive reader and alert churchman should be wary of the encroachment of government on the free exercise of religion in this country. It surfaces in many subtle and not so subtle ways.

Public schools have too often confused freedom of religion with freedom from religion. Zoning boards are making it harder and harder to build churches in desirable locations. Tax laws are being rewritten to try to attach some of the considerable capital that is vested in religious establishments within America.

It may not be long before this article will again have a more immediate relevance for American Christians.

> **XXII. Of Purgatory.** The Romish Doctrine concerning Purgatory, Pardons, Worshipping and Adoration, as well of Images as of Relics, and also Invocation of Saints, is a fond thing, vainly invented, and grounded upon no warranty of Scripture, but rather repugnant to the Word of God.

Because I am a person who is comfortable with the "gray" shades of life, I often wish there were a purgatory. The stark, vivid, and frighteningly eternal contrast between the felicity of heaven and the inferno of hell causes me great discomfort. Would that there was a middle ground, a *tertium quid*, a reformatory for wayward souls.

Purgatory, of course, was thought to be a place where those who had died were purged of sin and made ready for heaven. It was not thought to be a happy place, but it was a happy dogma, full of second chances and "try agains."

Of course, it was too good to be true. And, as such, it gave rise to a myriad of abuses. The practice of selling indulgences grew primarily because people could indulge themselves in sin and still buy back their souls. That is a crude over-simplification, but that was how it was seen by many.

The reformers would have none of it and denounced the whole concept in the strongest possible language. Yet, even that was not enough to keep John Henry Newman from finding some wiggle room in the statement. In his famous *Tract XC,* he decried the "Romish" doctrine while trying to uphold a more "catholic" doctrine of purgatory.

His creative parsing of the text in this one article went a long way toward discouraging the use of the Articles as a canon for the clergy. *Tract XC* is a reminder that if the will to do so is there, no phraseology is immune to deconstruction and dilution. As one social critic observed, we murder to dissect.

> **XXIII. Of Ministering in the Congregation.** It is not lawful for any man to take upon him the office of public preaching, or ministering the Sacraments in the Congregation, before he be lawfully called, and sent to execute the same. And those we ought to judge lawfully called and sent, which be chosen and called to this work by men who have public authority given unto them in the Congregation, to call and send Ministers into the Lord's vineyard.

The original intent of this article was to advise and warn the people against unauthorized ministers assuming control of congregations. The Anabaptists largely eschewed a concept of a regularized clergy opting instead for a less mediated, more charismatic and episodic form of leadership. The reformers wanted to "reform" the structures and doctrines of the Medieval Church, but they still believed in "form."

The issue has been both a bane and a blessing in America where, in the interest of maintaining a separation of church and state, the government has been very reluctant to define precisely who or what a "minister" is. With over 2,000 denominations in America, and with kilos more churches not tied to any denominational structure, the whole concept of who is authorized to perform religious services becomes a little like herding butterflies.

The article does articulate a helpful matrix, however. Buried in the language of the article are two words, repeated twice, that can go a long way toward clearing up confusion in this area: "called" and "sent."

Ministers of the Gospel, if they are to follow the Biblical pattern, must be both called and sent. Jesus called His disciples to Him and He sent them out to minister *in His name and under His authority.* The Great Commission begins with Jesus claiming that *"All authority in heaven and earth has been given me. Therefore, go . . ." (Matthew 28:18).*

The Church is composed of and led by those called out (one of the Greek words for church is *ekklesia* — from two smaller Greek words meaning to be "called out"). *"As Jesus was walking beside the Sea of Galilee, he saw two brothers, Simon called Peter and his brother Andrew. They were casting a net into the lake, for they were fishermen. . . . Going on from there, he saw two other brothers, James son of Zebedee and his brother John. They were in a boat with their father Zebedee, preparing their nets. Jesus called them . . . " (Matthew 4:18, 21).*

Once Jesus had called them, He also sent them. The Greek for this is a form of the word *apostle.* In *Matthew 10:16* and *Acts 26:17,* that is the term used. Jesus is saying, I am "apostleing" you.

A minister of the Gospel who is lawfully accredited by the Church and the governing authority of the state is one who is both called — by the Lord and by the local congregation — and sent — by the Godly authority to which he or she is openly and visibly accountable.

> **XXIV. Of Speaking in the Congregation in such a Tongue as the people understandeth.** It is a thing plainly repugnant to the Word of God, and the custom of the Primitive Church, to have public Prayer in the Church, or to minister the Sacraments, in a tongue not understanded of the people.

It may come as a shock to many that one of the founding principles of the Anglican Church is that it be "user-friendly." It had been the habit of the Medieval Church to use Latin for all its services. Most people did not speak or understand Latin (including many of the clergy who routinely and rotely rattled off the liturgy). This led to many abuses and misunderstandings. (Our word "hocus-pocus" is a parody of the Latin words for "This is my body," *hoc est corpus meum.*) The English Reformation set about to change that and to make the liturgy available to the common people not only geographically (more local parishes) and chronologically (by reducing the nine daily offices of prayer to two) but linguistically as well.

An honest question, with which Anglicans need to wrestle, is whether Elizabethan English still qualifies as "a tongue understanded of the people." Liturgy needs always to balance the need to be easily comprehended with the need to be a vehicle for the elevation and education of the people. This is no simple task and, as with most things, churches have tended to fall off on one side or the other — making worship and liturgy so "user-friendly" that it is as mundane and pedestrian as the latest popular song or, on the other hand, retaining forms and expressions that have become opaque to almost everyone except devotees of British costume dramas.

> **XXV. Of the Sacraments.** Sacraments ordained of Christ be not only badges or tokens of Christian men's profession, but rather they be certain sure witnesses, and effectual signs of grace, and God's good will towards us, by the which he doth work invisibly in us, and doth not only quicken, but also strengthen and confirm our Faith in him. There are two Sacraments ordained of Christ our Lord in the Gospel, that is to say, Baptism, and the Supper of the Lord. Those five commonly called Sacraments, that is to say, Confirmation, Penance, Orders, Matrimony, and Extreme Unction, are not to be counted for Sacraments of the Gospel, being such as have grown partly of the corrupt following of the Apostles, partly are states of life allowed in the Scriptures, but yet have not like nature of Sacraments with Baptism, and the Lord's Supper, for that they have not any visible sign or ceremony ordained of God. The Sacraments were not ordained of Christ to be gazed upon, or to be carried about, but that we should duly use them. And in such only as worthily receive the same, they have a wholesome effect or operation: but they that receive them unworthily, purchase to themselves damnation, as Saint Paul saith.

We now enter another complicated but crucial section of the Articles, that of the nature and power of the sacraments.

Being Latin, the word "sacrament" is not, strictly speaking, a Biblical word. It is not found in the Bible but is used to translate a Greek word μυστήριον, which we translate into a cognate: "mystery." Unfortunately, the meaning most people naturally attach to the word "mystery" is far afield from either what the Latin "sacrament" or the Greek μυστήριον meant.

When most people think of a mystery, they conjure up images of an Agatha Christie novel or a "Columbo" detective television show. Something has happened, usually bad, and the hero or heroine has a finite amount of time to figure out "who done it."

The Biblical concept of μυστήριον, or sacrament, is not about piecing togther evidence and catching an illusive and furtive subject. The Biblical concept is that of a sacred encounter with something that had previously been unknown but is now freely revealed. It does not have to be deciphered or decoded. It is not concealed, it is revealed.

The classic definition of a Biblical sacrament is that it is "an outward and visible sign of an inward and spiritual grace." To this, the Anglican Church has traditionally added a third element, that it be specifically ordained by Christ, Himself.

Thus, the Anglican Church recognizes two sacraments: Baptism and The Lord's Supper — the Eucharist. The Church freely recognizes that other activities may have sacramental components or be sacramental in nature, but they are not true Sacraments in the Biblical sense outlined above.

Both of the Biblical sacraments essentially symbolize the same thing, the death of Christ and the promise of new life in His sacrifice. The Greek word "baptize" means to immerse with the connotation that the item immersed is thoroughly soaked. Baptism does this by symbolically lowering the person into a watery grave (usually a *very* shallow one on a stand — so shallow that the water must be poured onto the person rather than the person being put into the water) and then raising them to new life in Christ. The action is a mini-reenactment of death and resurrection. "*We were therefore buried with him through baptism into death in order that, just as Christ was raised from the dead through the glory of the Father, we too may live a new life" (Romans 6:4).*

Jesus spoke of His death as a baptism and as a drinking of the cup: *"'You don't know what you are asking,' Jesus said. 'Can you drink the cup I drink or be baptized with the baptism I am baptized with?'"* (Mark 10:38). Thus, the communion is also a proclamation of the Lord's death: *"For whenever you eat this bread and drink this cup, you proclaim the Lord's death until he comes"* (I Corinthians 11:26).

The sacraments are not only "badges" or "tokens" of our commitment to God but are also, and primarily, "witnesses" and "effectual signs" of God's commitment to us. The sacraments are not something we do for God, they are reminders of what He has done, and continues to do "invisibly," for and in us. We are not to wear them as badges we have earned, nor display them as tokens which gain us entry into some state of blessedness. We are to regard them as witnesses and signs, and as such, they point beyond themselves — just as witnesses and signs do.

A "certain sure witness" is a trustworthy messenger, accurately describing a larger reality. A sign, if it is "effectual" must be clearly connected to the reality which it represents. A sign post that is turned askew or stolen and hung in an adolescent's bedroom no longer serves its function because, in the first case, it bears a false witness and, in the second, it is entirely removed from the reality to which it was intended to point.

The sacraments point us beyond themselves to God and to His Son's sacrifice on the Cross. If they are divorced from that context, or turned by careless or malicious hands, they are no longer sacraments of the Gospel.

Does that, then, mean that the efficacy of the sacraments depends on the good will of the person administering them?

> **XXVI. Of the Unworthiness of the Ministers, which hinders not the effect of the Sacraments.** Although in the visible Church the evil be ever mingled with the good, and sometimes the evil have chief authority in the Ministration of the Word and Sacraments, yet forasmuch as they do not the same in their own name, but in Christ's, and do minister by his commission and authority,

we may use their Ministry, both in hearing the Word of God, and in receiving the Sacraments. Neither is the effect of Christ's ordinance taken away by their wickedness, nor the grace of God's gifts diminished from such as by faith, and rightly, do receive the Sacraments ministered unto them; which be effectual, because of Christ's institution and promise, although they be ministered by evil men.

Nevertheless, it appertaineth to the discipline of the Church, that inquiry be made of evil Ministers, and that they be accused by those that have knowledge of their offences; and finally, being found guilty, by just judgment be deposed.

The answer to the question raised above regarding Article XXV is, "No." If that were the case, there would have only been one valid Lord's supper in all of human history. The reformers were conscious of the fact that in 16th century England parishioners were required by law to attend their local parishes on Sundays and, once there, to receive its ministrations. This created a problem for some sincere Christians because they knew their local ministers to be people of less than noble bearing. If the fellow preaching the sermon were a hypocrite, the thoughtful listener could sift out the wheat from the chaff. But, if the celebrant at the communion were a scoundrel, did that mean that the sacrament lost it validity?

This question went back at least as far as the controversy St. Augustine had with a group called the "Donatists." These sincere Christian people had broken off from the "mainline" Church during one of the great persecutions because the local "mainline" bishop had become a "traitor" to the faith.[121] They had handed over symbols of the faith to those who were persecuting them to avoid the hardships of the persecution. The Donatists maintained that the mainline had lost its pipeline to God.

Augustine disagreed and carried the day. Without condoning the actions of the cowardly bishops and priests, the Church condemned the Donatists as heretics because they located the authority of the sacraments in the person of the minister rather than in the character and *charis* (grace) of God.

---

121 Literally, a traditor — "one who hands over." Hence, our words "traitor" and "tradition" have the same root meaning, to hand something (or someone) over.

Thus, the faithful parishioner can rest easy knowing that it does not matter *sacramentally* if the celebrant at the local church has sin in his heart or soil on his hands.

Having said that, the first paragraph of this article cannot be taken in isolation from the second. Thus, it is incumbent upon the Church to thoroughly investigate and, if necessary, "depose" (remove from office) any minister who proves him or herself to be an unfit example and/or shepherd to the flock.

It is important to note that in the Pastoral Epistles, the qualifications given for those who aspire to offices in the Church have very little to do with abilities or gifts and a great deal to do with character and a goodly and Godly reputation in the community. (See, for example, *I Timothy 3 & Titus 1*.)

The article also presupposes that the minister is basically orthodox in his theology. This provision does not excuse heresy anymore than it excuses immorality. The early Christian Church viewed those who held doctrinal/theological opinions contrary to the orthodox Christian Faith as persons who were thereby outside of the Faith and outside the Church. . . .The reality was — as stated by Elert in "Eucharist and Church Fellowship in the First Four Centuries," "The early church was never in doubt that unity in doctrine is a prerequisite of altar fellowship. . . . Heterodoxy breaks the fellowship *ipso facto* . . . . The boundary runs between orthodoxy and heterodoxy. The hierarchical unity of the episcopate and orthodoxy are both criteria of the unity of the church. However, when these two come into collision, orthodoxy has the unqualified preeminence."

Finally, directly from the pen of John of Damascus: "We must maintain with all strength that the Eucharist is to be neither received from nor given to heretics."

Unless Article XXVI is taken in its entirety, it can too easily become a haven for rascals and a salve that heals God's people "slightly" (*Jeremiah 8:11*).

> **XXVII. Of Baptism.** Baptism is not only a sign of profession, and mark of difference, whereby Christian men are discerned from others that be not christened, but it is also a sign of Regen-

eration or New-Birth, whereby, as by an instrument, they that
receive Baptism rightly are grafted into the Church; the promises of the forgiveness of sin, and of our adoption to be the sons
of God by the Holy Ghost, are visibly signed and sealed, Faith
is confirmed, and Grace increased by virtue of prayer unto God.

The Baptism of young Children is in any wise to be retained
in the Church, as most agreeable with the institution of Christ.

The essential symbolism of the two sacraments was discussed
above; they both represent the believer's participation in the
death of Christ. But, each of the two sacraments raised specific
issues regarding efficacy and implementation.

In the 16th century (as also today), the question, "What happens when a person is baptized?" would have elicited responses
ranging from "He gets wet," to "She is made a joint heir with
Christ and guaranteed a place in heaven." How does the Episcopal Church answer this question? Some would say, all of the
above, none of the above, "I feel strongly both ways," or "Can
we talk about something less volatile, like, say, nuclear war?"

The Anglican Church has always tried to affirm both the veracity of God's promise and the necessity of personal faith. The
Baptism service has page after page of questions and affirmations
which the candidate and/or the sponsors must answer about
their own faith and their Godly intentions. If faith is present,
and if God's promises are remembered and invoked, then Baptism can be like the planting of a seed.[122]

I have asked this question to hundreds of people and had
some fun discussions as a result: "Is a seed alive?" Well, yes and
no. Seeds can live for millennia without sunlight, air, or water.
They do not, of themselves, reproduce, move, or grow. Yet, when
they are planted in the soil and furnished with light, water, and
nutrients, they do grow. It might be best to say that a seed has a
life dormant within it. So it is with Baptism. It is one sort of the
good seed of which Jesus spoke and, if it is given a chance, it
will grow and produce fruit.

Unfortunately, that is not always the case. Notice the little
phrase "they that receive Baptism rightly." What does it mean

---

122 This writer is grateful to his liturgics professor, Dr. Charles Price, for this analogy.

to receive baptism rightly? In faith. Faith in what? In baptism? No, faith in God's promise and Christ's offer of forgiveness. All too many sincere Christians believe what I call the vaccine view of baptism. In this view, the parents and/or sponsors don't have to understand or even participate in the vaccine. They just hand the child over to the person dressed in white, he or she squirts the kid, and whatever it was the kid had, he (or she) doesn't have it anymore.

The parents pay the bill and go home, relaxed in the belief that they don't have to do a thing — except to get the pictures developed and mailed to relatives and to keep track of the certificate in case they ever transfer churches.

Back to the analogy of a seed. There are tulip bulbs that cost hundreds of dollars. If I had such a bulb, I would not toss it out the kitchen window and hope it grew. For such a valuable seed I would make sure I learned everything I could about how to nourish and care for the seed. I would make sure it had the best location in which to grow. I would protect it from the evils that assail young plants.

The analogy is obvious. The seed sown in baptism is infinitely more valuable than any tulip bulb. Is it not clearly incumbent upon parents and godparents to see to it that the life for which they are stewards has the best possible chance to grow toward the Son? *"Train a child in the way he should go, and when he is old he will not turn from it" (Proverbs 22:6).*

The article also states, almost as an afterthought, that the baptism of young children is to be "retained." Infant baptism had been the practice of the Church from the earliest days (it is implied in *Acts 16* and, by analogy, in comparisons with circumcision in *Colossians 2:11-12*). Infant baptism was a hot topic in the 16th century. The very word "anabaptist" ("rebaptizer") refers to those who believed that infant baptism was invalid and needed to be repeated by the professing adult convert.

Both positions have problems. Infant baptism, if done in a careless, thoughtless, and faithless way, can lead to the assumption that becoming a Christian is simply a matter of ritual. So called "believer" baptism (or adult baptism) requires that the community of faith establishes an arbitrary age of accountabil-ity[123] and the fruit of "believer" baptism is no more consistent than that of infant baptism.

Given the fact that this was the practice of the ancient church, the Anglican Church has chosen to retain the practice. We do not go so far as to say that this particular method of baptism was specifically commanded by Christ. But we do believe that it is "agreeable with the institution of Christ."

> **XXVIII. Of the Lord's Supper.** The Supper of the Lord is not only a sign of the love that Christians ought to have among themselves one to another, but rather it is a Sacrament of our Redemption by Christ's death: insomuch that to such as rightly, worthily, and with faith, receive the same, the Bread which we break is a partaking of the Body of Christ; and likewise the Cup of Blessing is a partaking of the Blood of Christ. Transubstan-tiation (or the change of the substance of Bread and Wine) in the Supper of the Lord, cannot be proved by Holy Writ; but is repugnant to the plain words of Scripture, overthroweth the nature of a Sacrament, and hath given occasion to many super-stitions. The Body of Christ is given, taken, and eaten, in the Supper, only after an heavenly and spiritual manner. And the mean whereby the Body of Christ is received and eaten in the Supper, is Faith. The Sacrament of the Lord's Supper was not by Christ's ordinance reserved, carried about, lifted up, or wor-shipped.

Christians refer to this sacrament by two names, Holy Com-munion and Holy Eucharist. It is possible to see in these two names the two dimensions of the sacrament. "Holy" means "unique, set apart, special." The communion which Christians enjoy with each other and with the Lord around His table is sweet fellowship indeed. The word "communion" can be seen as refer-ring to the inter-personal dimension of the feast, not just on a human and temporal level but with the person of Jesus.

---

123 No "age of accountability" is given in Scripture. John the Baptist seemed to recog-nize Jesus while still in His mother's womb. This writer has seen children as young as four give a brief "testimony" of their conversion and be baptized as "believ-ers."

The word "eucharist" is the Greek word for "thanksgiving" and can be seen as a reference to the more "vertical" dimension of the feast, pointing the worshiper toward the crucified and ascended Christ. Anglicans call it "The Great Thanksgiving," and what could be greater than to give thanks for so great a gift?

As with baptism, Anglicans seek to affirm Christ's real presence in the feast without dissecting it in the process. The article walks that finest of lines — overtly and soundly denying "transubstantiation" while at the same time overtly and soundly denying pure "memorialism."

To understand what an educated and knowledgeable Roman Catholic means by "transubstantiation," one has to be acquainted with Aristotelian metaphysics and the difference between "substance" and "accident." (See the discussion above on Article I.) In brief, the Roman Catholic doctrine of transubstantiation teaches that at the eucharist, the *substance* of the bread and wine are *translated* into the substance of the body and blood of Christ. One should not expect to see the bread become flesh as it is consumed nor the wine become blood as it is drunk. The change would be invisible to the naked eye.

The Protestant Reformers rejected this understanding of the eucharist, finding that it was not plainly taught in Scripture and that it had "given occasion to many superstitions."

But the Anglican Reformers did not want to go so far as to say that nothing "real" happened in the eucharist. Christ was "really" present in some indescribable way. In the words of Queen Elizabeth's memorable little rhyme: "He took the bread and brake it, He was the Word that spake it, and what that Word did make it, I do believe and take it." Catchy but unsatisfying to those who seek absolute closure.

Think of it this way: once the pastor of another denomination tried to convince me that there was nothing more to the communion than a memorial. That the communion service was simply a mnemonic device, a memory aid, which Jesus had given His disciples. To illustrate his point, he took out his wallet and showed me a picture of his family. He said, "This is my family. Now, when I say that, I don't really mean my family is a piece of cardboard with colors on it. I mean this represents my family.

That is what Jesus was saying when He said, 'This is my body.' It was purely symbolic.'"

"Okay," says I. "Suppose I took that piece of cardboard out of your wallet and tore it up and stomped it into the ground. What would you do?"

"I'd slug you," he said.

"Why?" says I. "According to you, it's nothing but a piece of cardboard with no real value."

"Oh," he said, "I see your point."

Jesus gave us communion with the admonition: "... *do this in remembrance of me" (Luke 22:19).* That can mean two things, and it probably does: Do this because you remember — Do this and you will remember.

The article also reminds us that Christ commanded us to eat and drink the sacrament, not to worship it. That is why *The Book of Common Prayer* explicitly states that unless the bread and wine is being reserved for a specific and fairly immediate need, the elements should be "reverently" consumed (see the rubrics, *BCP* p. 408, 409). The perpetual "reservation" of the bread and/ or wine is not a traditional Anglican practice and raises serious questions about the very nature of the eucharist.

> **XXIX. Of the Wicked, which eat not the Body of Christ in the use of the Lord's Supper.** The Wicked, and such as be void of a lively faith, although they do carnally and visibly press with their teeth (as Saint Augustine saith) the Sacrament of the Body and Blood of Christ; yet in no wise are they partakers of Christ: but rather, to their condemnation, do eat and drink the sign or Sacrament of so great a thing.

It is incumbent upon any priest of the Church to discern whether any person within his or her charge is leading a "notoriously evil life." (*BCP* p. 409) The priest is to lovingly but firmly confront such a person and urge them to repent and be absolved before they present themselves for communion.[124] (See also Article XXXIII.)

---

124 This, by the way, is why the Confession, Absolution, and Passing of the Peace occur just before the Great Thanksgiving in the Episcopal worship service. *"Therefore, if you are offering your gift at the altar and there remember that your brother has something against you, leave your gift there in front of the altar. First go and be reconciled to your brother; then come and offer your gift" (Matthew 5:23-24).*

If an unrepentantly "wicked" or faithless person does come to communion, this article teaches that such a person does not receive the blessings and/or the grace available in the sacrament.

One is reminded of the Last Supper and how, even as he took the bread directly from the hand of Jesus, Judas received another spirit: "*As soon as Judas took the bread, Satan entered into him. 'What you are about to do, do quickly,' Jesus told him*" (*John 13:27*). One worries that sometimes Christians take communion too lightly. Perhaps a reading of the "Exhortation" on pages 316 and 317 of *The Book of Common Prayer* should be a more regular part of the liturgy.

> **XXX. Of both Kinds.** The Cup of the Lord is not to be denied to the Lay-people: for both the parts of the Lord's Sacrament, by Christ's ordinance and commandment, ought to be ministered to all Christian men alike.

It had become the custom in the Medieval Church to distribute the communion only in the form of the bread to the laity. The custom arose out of an overly-scrupulous desire not to defame the sacrament by accidentally spilling the wine during the distribution.

There is a sense in which this does not diminish the effect of the sacrament because Christ is fully communicated in either element. But, the reformers rightly discerned that to deny lay-persons the wine is to withhold a strong symbol of Christ's sacrifice. When possible, communion ought always to be of both bread and wine.

> **XXXI. Of the one Oblation of Christ finished upon the Cross.** The Offering of Christ once made is that perfect redemption, propitiation, and satisfaction, for all the sins of the whole world, both original and actual; and there is none other satisfaction for sin, but that alone. Wherefore the sacrifices of Masses, in the which it was commonly said, that the Priest did offer Christ for the quick and the dead, to have remission of pain or guilt, were blasphemous fables, and dangerous deceits.

An "oblation" is a sacrifice. This article was intended to argue against the Medieval Church's contention that the priest was, in a sense, re-sacrificing Christ at the eucharist. Christ died once for all[125] and His work was finished on the cross.

The founder of *Young Life*, an outreach ministry to high school and junior high aged young people, was a fellow named Jim Rayburn. As he lay dying of cancer, he called one of his young associates to him and handed him an envelope on which he had written these words: "The finished work of Christ — redemption, reconciliation, justification, atonement, propitiation, forgiveness, satisfaction . . ."

"Mitch," he said, "Never let 'em stop talking about Jesus."

Jesus is not only the author, He is the perfecter of our faith (*Hebrews 12:12*).

> **XXXII. Of the Marriage of Priests.** Bishops, Priests, and Deacons, are not commanded by God's Law, either to vow the estate of single life, or to abstain from marriage: therefore it is lawful for them, as for all other Christian men, to marry at their own discretion, as they shall judge the same to serve better to godliness.

Many a clergyperson who has not looked at the Articles in years are grateful that this article was included. While the Apostle Paul seems to make a case for the advantages of staying single (see *I Corinthians 7:8, 32, 33*), and while Jesus was single, it was clear that Peter was married (he had a mother-in-law) and that the practice of virtually every church except the Roman Church is to allow married clergy.

As a married person with three wonderful children, I can affirm that being married is a fulfilling and empowering calling within the Christian life (as well as the source of terrific sermon illustrations). A family is also, in Martin Luther's vivid phrase, the best "school for character" on the planet. But, we must also acknowledge that singleness can also be a fulfilling calling for the Christian. The sweetness of fellowship with the triune God and with God's people is enough for those who are called to that

---

125 *"Unlike the other high priests, he does not need to offer sacrifices day after day, first for his own sins, and then for the sins of the people. He sacrificed for their sins once for all when he offered himself" (Hebrews 7:27, see also Hebrews 9:12 and 26.).*

life. There is also a freedom in being unmarried that, once yielded to Him, God can use in marvelous ways.

> **XXXIII. Of excommunicate Persons, how they are to be avoided.** That person which by open denunciation of the Church is rightly cut off from the unity of the Church, and excommunicated, ought to be taken of the whole multitude of the faithful, as an Heathen and Publican, until he be openly reconciled by penance, and received into the Church by a Judge that hath authority thereunto.

The "heathen" were those on the "heath" who had not yet been instructed in Godly living. "Publicans," a term from the New Testament, were those who had openly turned their backs on their community to serve another god, another master.

The practice of "ex-communication" is rarely used. The easy availability of dozens of different Church communions in our mobile society has tended to make the disciplinary sanctions of any one communion virtually useless. The diminution of the Church's perceived authority in the world (especially the western world) has made a mockery of the Church's opprobrium. It was not always so.

This article dates to a time when the Church's moral authority was absolute. To be cut off from communion was not just to be cut off from a particular fellowship, it was to be cut off from "the means of grace and the hope of glory."

The Godly Church never wielded this tremendous power for purely punitive purposes. The goal was not the gaol, but that the person thus removed from the protective grace of the Christian community might be brought to repentance and restored.

"Timothy, my son, I give you this instruction in keeping with the prophecies once made about you, so that by following them you may fight the good fight, holding on to faith and a good conscience. Some have rejected these and so have shipwrecked their faith. Among them are Hymenaeus and Alexander, whom I have handed over to Satan to be taught not to blaspheme" (I Timothy 1:18-20).

Note that the article makes it clear that it is the person him or herself who has, by their own actions, separated themselves from the visible body of Christ. It is their "open denunciation of the Church" that has cut them off from the same. The hope and prayer of the Church must remain that such a person repent. Upon their repentance, some form of public demonstration of that repentance (referred to as penance) should be expected. Once that is done, the person may, and should, be restored to the full fellowship of the Church — amid rejoicing appropriate to the good news that a prodigal has come home.

> **XXXIV. Of the Traditions of the Church.** It is not necessary that Traditions and Ceremonies be in all places one, or utterly like; for at all times they have been divers, and may be changed according to the diversity of countries, times, and men's manners, so that nothing be ordained against God's Word. Whosoever, through his private judgment, willingly and purposely, doth openly break the Traditions and Ceremonies of the Church, which be not repugnant to the Word of God, and be ordained and approved by common authority, ought to be rebuked openly, (that others may fear to do the like,) as he that offendeth against the common order of the Church, and hurteth the authority of the Magistrate, and woundeth the consciences of the weak brethren. Every particular or national Church hath authority to ordain, change, and abolish, Ceremonies or Rites of the Church ordained only by man's authority, so that all things be done to edifying.

A friend of mine is doing mission work among a people group within a third world country. Over 90% of these half million people have never heard the name of Jesus. These people are beloved of God yet they do not know the Gospel of that love, so one of the tasks he has set himself is to translate portions of the *BCP* into their language. When I asked him why he would bother, he gave me a big grin and said, without hesitation, "Article thirty-four!"

At the time the Articles were originally written, at the time of their establishment in America, and again now as the cultures of the world are interacting as never before, it was clear that one size would not fit all.

In the latter part of the 16th century, the British empire was beginning its expansion to the ends of the earth. Within 100 years, the sun would never set on the peoples and places that came under its sway. Wherever it went, it took the Gospel with it and planted churches of the Anglican Communion. It was obvious that "traditions and ceremonies" would necessarily be different in different places. The Articles took that into consideration. So long as the doctrine of the Church was not altered, the manner of its expression was up to the local Church leadership.

The same thing happened in the American frontier and the same thing is happening even as this book is being written and read. As one person wisely said, "The two dangers are that we will change our message and that we won't change our methods."

The liturgy and music that worked well in an 18th century English village had little chance of working nearly as well in an 18th century African village. Similarly, the liturgy and music that "worked" well among suburban, middle class "anglos" of 1950's America has little chance of "working" with urbanized (or rural or immigrant or migrant or . . .) Hispanic (or Latvian or Native American or Asian or . . . you name it) peoples.

The Anglican Church has known this for centuries and is committed (on paper at least) to proclaiming the Gospel in such a way that it can be heard. In this sense, the Anglican Church is the greatest of all missionary churches.

> **XXXV. Of the Homilies.** The Second Book of Homilies, the several titles whereof we have joined under this Article, doth contain a godly and wholesome Doctrine, and necessary for these times, as doth the former Book of Homilies, which were set forth in the time of Edward the Sixth; and therefore we judge them to be read in Churches by the Ministers, diligently and distinctly, that they may be understood of the people.

Of the Names of the Homilies.
1) Of the right Use of the Church.
2) Against Peril of Idolatry.
3) Of repairing and keeping clean of Churches.
4) Of good Works: first of Fasting.
5) Against Gluttony and Drunkenness.
6) Against Excess of Apparel.

7) Of Prayer.

8) Of the Place and Time of Prayer.

9) That Common Prayers and Sacraments ought to be ministered in a known tongue.

10) Of the reverend Estimation of God's Word.

11) Of Alms-doing.

12) Of the Nativity of Christ.

13) Of the Passion of Christ.

14) Of the Resurrection of Christ.

15) Of the worthy receiving of the Sacrament of the Body and Blood of Christ.

16) Of the Gifts of the Holy Ghost.

17) For the Rogation-days.

18) Of the State of Matrimony.

19) Of Repentance.

20) Against Idleness.

21) Against Rebellion.

(This Article is received in this Church, so far as it declares the Books of Homilies to be an explication of Christian doctrine, and instructive in piety and morals. But all references to the constitution and laws of England are considered as inapplicable to the circumstances of this Church; which also suspends the order for the reading of said Homilies in churches, until a revision of them may be conveniently made, for the clearing of them, as well from obsolete words and phrases, as from the local references.)

Archbishop Cranmer was desperately concerned that the people of the nascent Anglican Church receive proper instruction in good and Godly doctrine. He had inherited a Church with a clergy that was largely ill-educated, ill-paid, and ill-motivated. Many could not be trusted to teach sound doctrine. People were coming to the Church for spiritual bread. He would not allow an ill-equipped clergy to feed them stones.

To that end, Cranmer and others composed and promulgated a series of "Homilies" on various essential Christian doctrines. These were to be read to the people for their instruction and edification. They are still good reading today.

XXXVI. Of Consecration of Bishops and Ministers. The Book of Consecration of Bishops, and Ordering of Priests and Deacons, as set forth by the General Convention of this Church in 1792, doth contain all things necessary to such Consecration and Ordering; neither hath it any thing that, of itself, is superstitious and ungodly. And, therefore, whosoever are consecrated or ordered according to said Form, we decree all such to be rightly, orderly, and lawfully consecrated and ordered.

The original 1571, 1662 text of this Article reads as follows: "The Book of Consecration of Archbishops and Bishops, and Ordering of Priests and Deacons, lately set forth in the time of Edward the Sixth, and confirmed at the same time by authority of Parliament, doth contain all things necessary to such Consecration and Ordering: neither hath it any thing, that of itself is superstitious and ungodly. And therefore whosoever are consecrated or ordered according to the Rites of that Book, since the second year of the forenamed King Edward unto this time, or hereafter shall be consecrated or ordered according to the same Rites; we decree all such to be rightly, orderly, and lawfully consecrated and ordered."

This article mandated an orderly passing on of orders. The concept of "Holy Orders" (that there should be a group of people set apart by proper authority for the leadership of the Church) goes back to the New Testament. (See also Article XXIII.)

XXXVII. Of the Power of the Civil Magistrates. The Power of the Civil Magistrate extendeth to all men, as well Clergy as Laity, in all things temporal; but hath no authority in things purely spiritual. And we hold it to be the duty of all men who are professors of the Gospel, to pay respectful obedience to the Civil Authority, regularly and legitimately constituted.

The original 1571, 1662 text of this Article reads as follows: "The King's Majesty hath the chief power in this Realm of England, and other his Dominions, unto whom the chief Government of all Estates of this Realm, whether they be Ecclesiastical or Civil, in all causes doth appertain, and is not, nor ought to be, subject to any foreign

Jurisdiction. Where we attribute to the King's Majesty the chief government, by which Titles we understand the minds of some slanderous folks to be offended; we give not our Princes the ministering either of God's Word, or of the Sacraments, the which thing the Injunctions also lately set forth by Elizabeth our Queen do most plainly testify; but that only prerogative, which we see to have been given always to all godly Princes in holy Scriptures by God himself; that is, that they should rule all estates and degrees committed to their charge by God, whether they be Ecclesiastical or Temporal, and restrain with the civil sword the stubborn and evil-doers. The Bishop of Rome hath no jurisdiction in this Realm of England. The Laws of the Realm may punish Christian men with death, for heinous and grievous offences. It is lawful for Christian men, at the commandment of the Magistrate, to wear weapons, and serve in the wars."

The reformers delineated three spheres of sovereignty within God's world: the family, the Church, and the state. While each overlaps the others in many ways, each sphere retains its own sovereignty under God. Paul was a Jew and a Roman citizen — a fact he used to his advantage on at least one occasion (*Acts 22:25ff*). Christian clergy and lay people are subject to all three spheres in their just and proper order.

This article simply stipulates that the common law of the land extends to all people, even clergy and laity, in "things temporal." In other words, clergy must obey speed limit signs, pay their taxes, etc. They do not have "diplomatic immunity" as citizens of another country, even if it is a heavenly one.

Churches must conform to local building codes and so on. This is as it should be for churches are full members of the community.

The quasi separation of Church and state in America has produced some interesting gray areas, though. Clergy do pay taxes, but the taxes are computed differently than for lay people. If a church catches fire, the first call is not usually to the diocese for assistance, it is to the local fire department — even though the Church as an institution does not pay taxes. As western society becomes more secularized, watch for these time-honored loopholes to close within the first few decades of the next century.

> **XXXVIII. Of Christian Men's Goods, which are not common.** The Riches and Goods of Christians are not common, as touching the right, title, and possession of the same; as certain Anabaptists do falsely boast. Notwithstanding, everyman ought, of such things as he possesseth, liberally to give alms to the poor, according to his ability.

This article and the next were written against some of the perceived errors of the Anabaptists. A cursory reading of *Acts 2-5* might lead one to believe that communal living and communal property were the norm for the early Christians. Some Anabaptists sought to emulate this model and, (here comes the rub) enforce it as normative.

This article states that while Christian charity is the duty of every Christian person, and that each person should give "liberally" and "according to his ability," such giving should be entirely voluntary and not coerced or legally binding.

The safest rule for Christians is probably John Wesley's simple formula: "Earn all you can, save all you can, give all you can."

> **XXXIX. Of a Christian Man's Oath.** As we confess that vain and rash Swearing is forbidden Christian men by our Lord Jesus Christ, and James his Apostle, so we judge, that Christian Religion doth not prohibit, but that a man may swear when the Magistrate requireth, in a cause of faith and charity, so it be done according to the Prophet's teaching in justice, judgment, and truth.

This may seem to be an odd statement to include in a church's confession of faith. But, the keeping of one's word is at the heart of the Gospel. Our salvation itself is based on God's promise to His people. And our Lord's brother, when he was casting about for the most important moral attribute in his homily to the Church (known to us as the Book of James) said this: *"Above all, my brothers, do not swear — not by heaven or by earth or by anything else. Let your 'Yes' be yes, and your 'No,' no, or you will be condemned."* (James 5:12)

The Anabaptists and some others felt that to take an oath was to imply that one was not always being truthful. And while that could be the inference, it is clearly not the intent. Having said that, those who would raise this as an issue of conscience may be on to something.

The world is crying out for people who will stand by their word. Integrity is consistently the highest value in the workplace, above competence, education, or good vacation plans. Christians above all other people are in a position to give a truly positive witness to the holiness and justice of God. The non-believers with whom we interact may not understand the nuances of the Trinity, the magnificence of the Atonement, or the enthusiams of the gifts of the Holy Spirit, but they will understand that if someone consistently keeps his or her word, that person is on to something special. As Psalm 15 says:

> *"Lord, who may dwell in your sanctuary?*
> *Who may live on your holy hill?*
>
> *He whose walk is blameless*
> *and who does what is righteous,*
> *who speaks the truth from his heart*
> *and has no slander on his tongue*
> *who does his neighbor no wrong*
> *and casts no slur on his fellowman,*
> *who despises a vile man*
> *but honors those who fear the Lord,*
> *who keeps his oath*
> *even when it hurts. . ."*

❈ E · I · G · H · T ❧

Conclusions

> There is, however, no future for undogmatic Christianity that
> is, for a Christianity — that follows wherever the thoughts of its
> current theological leaders may lead — because Christianity is es-
> sentially, and always has been historically, a dogmatic religion. . . .
> A religion of revelation which is given in the events and words of
> history must be dogmatic in character.
>
> David Broughton Knox

Hezekiah became the King of Judah at age 25. He was determined to return the people to the pure worship of the LORD. His
reforms included removing places of occult worship, "smash-
ing" sacred stones and cutting down the "Asherah poles" which
were the objects of pagan worship. To that point, his was a textbook, boiler-plate reformation. But, then he did something that
must have seemed sacrilegious in the extreme: "He broke into
pieces the bronze snake Moses had made."

How could a young King dare to destroy such an ancient
object, one which had been built at the command of God Himself and had been used so effectively by Him in the past? What
on earth (or in heaven!) could have prompted him to do such a
thing? The text itself provides the answer: *"Up to that time the
Israelites had been burning incense to it. (It was called
Nehushtan)"* (II Kings 18:1-4). The snake had become an idol. Its
name betrayed the dichotomy: *Nehushtan* meant both "bronze
snake" and "unclean thing."

God had been pleased to use the snake in the past as "a means
of grace." But, its usefulness (except as a museum piece) was
long gone. Hezekiah made a bold decision. He decided that, no

141

matter how valuable or grace-filled something had been in the past, if its presence in the life of God's people was hindering their worship, it needed to be gotten rid of. That is lesson number one.

Lesson number two, though, is that Hezekiah was *not* willing to get rid of the precepts God had given through Moses: *"He" [Hezekiah] held fast to the Lord and did not cease to follow him; he kept the commands the* LORD *had given Moses"* (*II Kings 18:6*). The snake could go. The snake needed to go. The law needed to stay. The snake was *adiaphora* but it had become an idol. The covenant law was essential but it was being neglected.

By analogy, this story raises an honest (and embarrassingly obvious) question: Are the Articles the snake or the law?

Some would say they are the snake: powerful symbols of God's mighty deeds from long ago and far away. As valuable as they once were, they are now getting in the way of true worship. To keep them around at all is to invite idle minds to idol worship. A. G. Dickens was right to refer to them as a "rather heavy clutter of anachronisms" for which there "remains a lingering, superstitious reverence."[126]

Yet, there are those of us who believe that the Articles have much more in common with the covenant law which Hezekiah jealously guarded than they do with the snake which he smashed. The Articles remain clear, concise, and time-honored statements of Anglican orthodoxy. If they ever were true (and if they weren't, the Anglican Church has a lot of explaining to do), then they still contain and convey Truth about God, humanity, salvation, and grace.

In His grace, God brings us moments when we can choose how we will respond to His self-revelation. We began this study with a quick review of the covenant renewal that took place when Josiah was King of Judah. Josiah lived in an age when monarchs were viewed as just that — the "one source" (the literal meaning of the Greek word *mon-arche*). The word of the king was absolute. But it was not a dream or a vision or an ecstatic celestial

---

126 Dickens, p. 252.

intervention that turned Josiah's will. He was simply confronted by the words of the sacred text. The words changed him and, through him, the society of the people of God.

The good news is that, for a season, the people of God had their faith reinvigorated, revitalized, and reformed. The bad news is that the reformation did not last long — they never do. That is why they must be reaffirmed and renewed.

On this side of heaven, even our best and most faithful responses to God, even our most cherished institutions, are subject to fairly rapid decay. That is why there is a desperate need at this time to do a radical theological self-examination — "radical" meaning, quite literally, from the root. As John the Baptist said, the axe is laid at the root of the tree.

The other good news is that, just in Josiah's day, there is still power in a Godly text. The need for the Articles as a rule and guide is critical for today's church and the church that will emerge in the 21st century (if the Lord tarries). Yes, the Articles are an "Historical Document." So is the *Constitution*, the *Magna Carta*, and the sacred Scriptures. In an age when the discipline of history itself is out of favor with most people in the pew, to intentionally saddle such lively and life-giving documents with the moniker "historical" is misleading and prejudicial.

On a more "pseudo-sophisticated" level, one is reminded of the cynical archeological ditty: "There are no facts, just artifacts." For many in this camp, the Articles are an "artifact," no more lively than a lump of clay, dusted off, carefully labeled and displayed under glass in a museum. But, like it or not, they *are* a fact. They *are* the standing statement of the doctrine of the Episcopal Church. When we open up the tomb, as we have done in this book, we see that the Articles were, quite literally, buried alive.

Should we go so far as Dr. Bromiley when he suggested that one honest way of treating the Articles was to bury them formally and finally? The notion accords with nobility; Anglicans love a good funeral. Yet, I believe we should choose life. I propose that, having shuffled them out the back door in the dead of night like unwelcome and unseemly house guests, we invite these old friends back in, this time through the front door.

The Episcopal Church has not in the past required, nor should it now require, "conformity" to the Articles but it should require that the Articles be "acknowledged" and "honored." A denomination that prides itself on its willingness to *think* and its unashamed confidence in "reason" dare not refuse to think through and declare its beliefs clearly and precisely.

Why should we now, at this late date, lament their deletion from the Constitution and their placement in what Bromiley has called "the basement" of *The Book of Common Prayer*?[127] And what would be the benefit of bringing this "rather heavy clutter of anachronisms," this "Christian text from the past,"[128] with us into the 21st century?

The re-establishment and honoring of the Articles is crucial to the vitality (*if not the mortality*) of the Anglican Church. It is more than an "academic" issue. If the Episcopal Church is to respond wisely, effectively, and faithfully to the challenges that lie ahead, if we are to have anything of substance to say to the culture around us, we must honor and protect the Articles as a worthy and, indeed, necessary starting point for pastoral, theological, and ecclesiastical dialogue.

Why should we honor the Articles? For at least three reasons:

First, we should honor the Articles for our neighbors in other faith communities. It honors our neighbors when we are careful to present our core convictions in a clear and unambiguous fashion. There are literally millions of souls out there, men and women for whom Christ died, who sincerely want to understand what our Church believes. We owe it to their honest inquiry to offer honest answers. And our answers must not be wrapped in arcane Anglican jargon or buried in a liturgy that has more options and variations than an American shopping mall.

Second, we should honor the Articles for those within our communion. It honors our unique calling within the Body of Christ when those who have chosen to identify themselves as Anglican Christians can also identify what that means in an ar-

---

127 Bromiley, "A Curious Anniversary," p. 5.

128 O'Donovan, p. 7.

ticulate and winsome way. The various Anglican Prayer Books are used by a wide range of Christian people for devotion, for guidance, and for education. The use of the liturgy alone does not make them Anglicans. Nor do the outward signs of Baptism or Confirmation. The Episcopal Church is not mentioned in either the Baptism or the Confirmation office by name. True membership is not found in legal or sentimental ties to Canterbury. What identifies Anglicans as Anglicans is a thoughtful and self-conscious commitment to a certain way of following Christ. That way is most completely and honestly articulated in the Articles.

Finally, we should honor the Articles because it honors God when we love Him with our minds. Even as we recognize that questioning and paradox are part of the mystery of faith and how we now see in a mirror dimly, we also affirm that the striving for clarity and conviction is pleasing to a God whose incarnate Son commended His followers to seek the Truth.

To that end, I make the following modest proposals: (A) Restore the Articles to their rightful place in Article X of The Constitution. (B) In the next edition of the *BCP*, take them out of the "basement" and make them a part of the catechism. (C) Pass a resolution at the General Convention in the year 2000 (on the eve of the 200th anniversary of their "establishment") giving them a "primacy of honor" in matters of doctrine similar to that extended to the Archbishop of Canterbury in matters episcopal. (D) Establish a committee composed of representatives from each Episcopal seminary and Bishops from each province, to revise the Articles by the year 2001, in time for the 200th anniversary of their establishment as the official doctrinal statement of our Church.

I remember my two friends — the woman who could have cared less about theology and the man who was trying to care but who let an uninformed "spiritual guide" inform his caring. Then I remember King Josiah. My great hope is that someday a Hilkiah will bring out these laws from some dusty corner of a seminary library basement. And then he will dare to read them before the people. And these people, and thousands like them, will rise up and say "Why didn't you tell us?" Why, indeed?

"Watch your life and doctrine closely. Persevere in them, because if you do, you will save both yourself and your hearers" (*I Timothy 4:16*).

Discussion Questions

1)   Do you agree with David Knox's comment that there is "no future for undogmatic Christianity"? Why or why not?

2)   What are some sacred snakes in the Church today? How might they be "smashed" without violating the faith of the people?

3)   Do you think clergy should be held to a higher standard than lay people? In all areas of life? In doctrine and/or conduct only?

4)   In what ways might the restoration of the Articles be crucial to the mortality of the Episcopal Church? Its vitality? Can you think of any good reason not to restore the Articles?

A Glossary of
Important Terms and People

Act of Succession: Passed in 1534, it reaffirmed the independence of the Church of England from the Church in Rome and reinstated the English Crown as the controlling power (the exact title was still to be worked out) of the English Church.

Adiaphora: A semi-technical term denoting semi-important things. From the Greek, it means "things indifferent," in other words, those things about which people of a good and Godly faith should feel free to differ. It should be remembered, however, that one person's *adiaphora* may be another's chosen ditch in which to die.

Anabaptists (ism):   Literally "re-baptizers." "The comprehensive designation of various groups on the Continent who in the 16th century refused to allow their children to be baptized and reinstituted the baptism of believers." (from: *The Oxford Dictionary of the Christian Church*—"*ODCC*") These various groups, which ranged from charismatic enthusiasts to thoughtful monastics, were severely persecuted by the "mainline" reformers such as Luther, Calvin and Zwingli. Their witness lives on in movements such as the Mennonites, Amish, Moravians, Quakers, etc.

Antinomian(ism):   Literally "against [the] law." The conviction that Christians are set free from any obligation to keep the law or submit to authority.

Augsburg Confession: Perhaps the preeminent Protestant Creed of the early Reformation. It was written in 1530, largely by Philip Melanchthon, under the guidance of Martin Luther. Its intention was "To make the Lutheran position as inoffensive as possible to the Catholic party, its language was studiously moderate." (*ODCC*)

Bishops' Book: Published in 1537, it was also known as *The Institution (or Instruction) of a Christian Man*. It was an exposi-

147

tion of the Lord's Prayer, the Apostles' Creed, the Ten Commandments, and several other key texts of Christendom. Because it was never approved by the secular authorities, it was called the *Bishops' Book* to distinguish it from the *King's Book* (1543) which did gain secular approval.

"Bloody" Mary: (a) An alcoholic drink made with tomato juice; (b) the Queen of England from 1553 to 1558. Henry VIII's daughter by Catherine of Aragon. She tried to return England to Roman Catholicism. Her harsh efforts at "reform" soured the English people on radical religiosity of any stripe and set the stage for the moderate Reformation known as the Elizabethan Settlement and the birth of the Anglican Communion as we now know it.

Broad-Churchman(ship):   Essentially the conviction that conviction is not all it's cracked up to be. This term refers to a style of being Christian people that places a very high, if not quite ultimate, value on the acceptance of a wide variety of liturgical and theological convictions. It is sometimes also called **latitudinarianism**, a term that identifies this view as one that believes there is a wide "latitude" in what is acceptable doctrine, practice, etc.

It would be enticing, but wrong-headed and ill-mannered, to see in this view an oblique reference to Jesus' words in *Matthew 7:13: "Enter through the narrow gate. For wide is the gate and broad is the road that leads to destruction, and many enter through it."*

Calvin, John: (1509-1564) A French reformer and theologian who settled in Geneva and set about to reform the city and its churches along biblical lines. He was the author of numerous biblical commentaries still in wide use today and his *Institutes of the Christian Religion*, intended as a basic primer on the essentials of the Christian Faith, is a masterpiece of clear, reformed Protestant theology as it developed in the 16th century.

It is an unfortunate fact of history that many people have both loved and loathed Calvin without ever reading a single thing he wrote.

Calvinism: It might seem odd that a distinction needs to be drawn between John Calvin and the movement that bears his name, but such is the case. "Calvinism" takes many forms today. While almost all would self-consciously find their roots in the insights of John Calvin, Calvin himself would likely find many of the movements that bear his name to be inconsistent with the worshipful and moderate temper of his thought.

Catholic: The quality of being "universal" in scope. God's Church in God's world has universal claim on His world and a universal character within that world. Not to be confused with Roman Catholic, which refers to that part of the universal church which is overtly aligned with the Roman See. (See *"Roman Catholic"* below.)

Cranmer, Thomas: (b. 1489) Archbishop of Canterbury under Henry VIII, Edward VI, and briefly "Bloody" Mary. He was executed by Mary in 1556. He was the architect of the English Reformation and the author of *The Book of Common Prayer* and the first several versions of the Articles of Religion.

Edward VI: Son of Henry VIII by Jane Seymour. Acceded to throne at age nine after his father's death in 1547. During his reign, the country was guided by several "protectors" with overt Protestant leanings. This somewhat abrupt shift toward Protestantism set the stage for the "reforms" of "Bloody" Mary, who acceded to the throne at Edward's death in 1553.

Elizabethan I: (1555-1603) Queen of England from 1558. Daughter of Henry VIII and Anne Boleyn. Responsible for "Elizabethan Settlement" (see below).

Elizabethan Settlement: The name usually given to the series of events instituted by and at the request of Queen Elizabeth during the latter part of the 16th century that brought religious peace to England. The "settlement" steered a course which affirmed the basic tenets of Protestantism while maintaining a moderate reformation of practice, polity, and theology. The final approval of the Articles of Religion in the 1570's was a key element in effecting the settlement.

Evangelical (ism):   In an attempt to bring some focus to a rather fuzzy term, David Bebbington maintains that there are four essential characteristics that define "evangelicalism" "conversionism, activism, biblicism and crucicentrism." (Bebbington, *Evangelicalism in Modern Britain*, p. 4). In other words, Evangelicals are those who are self-consciously committed to the concepts

- that becoming a follower of Christ involves a decision of the will and a change of the heart (conversion),
- that Christian disciples should make a difference in the world (activism),
- that the Scriptures are the ultimate authority for faith and practice — in Wesley's words *homo unis libri "a man of one book"* (biblicism), and
- that the doctrine of the cross and the atonement are the central and essential fact around which the Christian faith revolves (crucicentrism).

Gnosticism: One of the earliest Christian heresies, present at the writing of the New Testament, which taught that it was only through a "secret knowledge" (*gnosis* = knowledge) that a disciple could progress in the faith.

Hooker, Richard: (c. 1554-1600) Archetypical Anglican divine whose most famous work, the seven volume *Laws of Ecclesiastical Policy* was published over a period of 68 years from 1594-1662. During his brief life he served as an instructor at Oxford and as a parish priest at several parishes in England. His public and scholarly disputations with the more Calvinistic Walter Travers (with whom he shared a pulpit at The Temple Church in London), helped to regularize and articulate classical Anglicanism's three-fold theological emphasis on Scripture, Tradition, and Reason.

Institution of a Christian Man: Following the *Ten Articles* of 1536, it was the second attempt by Thomas Cranmer to craft a document stating the unique theological distinctives of the renewed Church of England.

King's Book: *aka* "A Necessary Doctrine and Erudition for any Christian Man," published in 1543 at the direction of Henry VIII.

Based on the "Bishops' Book" of 1537, it reasserted in stronger terms the royal supremacy while it also maintained a substantially Roman Catholic theology. Thomas Cranmer probably helped craft this document.

Luther, Martin: (1483-1546) Almost certainly the most significant single figure of the Protestant Reformation and one of the most towering figures in all of human history. A German monk and scholar whose celebrated struggles to find holiness in the context of the Medieval Christianity led him to rediscover the central biblical truths that salvation is a gift, given by God's grace and received by faith alone. His insights into the nature of Christian vocation, the priesthood of all believers, the nature of civil vs ecclesiastical government, and the nature of sanctification in the context of a real world full of real people changed the whole economy and politics of the Western world.

His cause was aided by the presence of the printing press, the rise of nation states, and his ability to use both to his advantage.

Marburg Colloquy: Called by Philip of Hesse in 1529, it was an attempt to bring unity between the Saxon and Swiss Reformers. Luther, Melanchthon, Ulrich Zwingli, and Martin Bucer attended. Though the conference failed to produce any truly substantial agreements among the reformers, it did issue a document that Luther and Melanchthon used as the basis for the Augsburg Confession.

Melanchthon, Phillip: (1497-1560) A scholar of the Renaissance who helped shape the Reformation. While he was Luther's lieutenant, he was also a significant figure in his own right whose love of learning and whose gift with language served the Reformation well.

He was the major architect and author of the Augsburg Confession and his commentaries on the scripture took the insights of the classics and of the nascent and emerging science of archaeology into serious consideration.

Oxford Movement: "The movement (1833-1845) within the Church of England, centered at Oxford, which aimed at restoring the High Church ideals of the 17th century. . . Among the more immediate causes were the fear that the [Roman] Catholic Emancipation Act (1829) would lead many Anglicans into the Roman Catholic Church, the anxiety occasioned by the passing of the Reform Bill (1832) and the plan to suppress ten Irish bishoprics. . . Its chief object was the defense of the Church of England as a Divine Institution, of the doctrine of Apostolic Succession, and of the *BCP* as a rule of faith." (*ODCC*)

Pelagianism: "Theologically, Pelagianism is the heresy which holds that man can take the initial and fundamental steps toward salvation by his own efforts, apart from Divine Grace." (*ODCC*) It is named after one of its earliest proponents, a fellow named Pelagius (born about 370) who engaged in a lively dialogue with St. Augustine about the nature of sin. Augustine's view prevailed and has been considered the "orthodox" view ever since.

Protestant (ism):   A very hard word to define. The scrupulous reader is referred to a good theological dictionary. In the meantime, these brief excerpts from the *ODCC*'s entry will have to do.

"The system of Christian faith and practice based on acceptance of the principles of the Reformation. . . . The chief characteristics of original Protestantism, common to all its denominations, are the acceptance of the Bible as the only source of revealed truth, the doctrine of justification by faith only, and the universal priesthood of all believers."

Reformed: Another hard-to-define word. Broadly speaking, it refers to those beliefs and practices which grew out of, or are identified with, the Reformation, especially on the Protestant side. The word is often used by those outside of Protestantism as a synonym for "Protestant" (which it sometimes is) but when used by those within Protestantism it is used as a nuanced reference to the more Calvinistic followers of the Reformation.

Roman Catholic: That part of the one Holy Catholic and Apostolic Church which is overtly aligned with the Roman See and looks to the Bishop of Rome as its head on earth.

Ten Articles: Written by Cranmer and distributed in 1536, two years after the Act of Succession. It was a compromise document between Protestants and Catholics attempting to state the basic theological position(s) of the renewed English Church.

Thirteen Articles: In the aftermath of Henry VIII's excommunication by the Pope in 1538, Cranmer made this early attempt to develop a statement of faith that was congenial to Lutherans and other moderate Continental Reformers.

White, Bp. William: (1748-1836) In many ways the architect of The Protestant Episcopal Church in United States of America (PECUSA). In 1787, he became the second person to be consecrated as an American bishop. His influence was due to his wisdom, foresight, and longevity. Still active even in his 87th year, William White participated in the consecration of 27 American bishops. By contrast, Samuel Seabury, the first American bishop and a frequent protagonist to White, died in 1796 having only participated in the consecration of one American bishop and Samuel Provoost, the third American bishop died in 1815 and only helped consecrate six more bishops.

Time Line

50-100 Christianity somehow comes to the British Isles, perhaps brought by Roman soldiers on deployment.

460 St. Patrick dies after having returned to Ireland as a Christian missionary bishop.

596 Augustine of Canterbury is sent by Pope Gregory the Great as a missionary to the people of *Angle-Land*.

664 Synod of Whitby at which the Church in England formally ties itself to the Church in Rome.

1384 John Wyclife, early English reformer, dies.

1492 Columbus sails the ocean blue and opens a "new world" to European civilization.

1517 Luther nails his "95 Theses" to the door of the Wittenberg church.

1521 Diet of Worms and Luther is officially labeled a heretic.

1529 Marburg Colloquy.

1530 Augsburg Confession is distributed.

1533 Thomas Cranmer accedes to the Archbishop of Canterbury.

1534 Act of Supremacy wherein the English Crown reasserts control of the English Church.

1536 Ten Articles distributed.

Thomas Cromwell tries continually to get Henry VIII to align politically with Germany.

Henry VIII invites three German Protestant theologians to England for consultation with Cranmer and other English theologians.

William Tyndale executed in Brussels on orders from Henry VIII and Thomas More.

1537 *Institution of a Christian Man* (a.k.a. *The Bishops' Book*) is distributed.

1538	Henry VIII is excommunicated by the Pope.
	Thirteen Articles are drawn up as a result of consultation with the Lutherans.
	The Royal Commission stigmatizes Anabaptists.
1543	*Necessary Doctrine and Erudition for Any Christian Man* (a.k.a. the *King's Book*) is published.
1546	Luther dies.
1547	Henry VIII dies and Edward VI accedes to the throne.
1549	First English *BCP*.
1552	Second *BCP*.
1553	First Complete set of *Articles*, 42 in all, is published.
	Edward dies, "Bloody" Mary accedes.
1556	Cranmer, Ridley, Latimer, and many other reformers die in the flames.
1558	Mary dies, Elizabeth I accedes to the throne.
1559	Third *BCP*.
1571	Final English version of the Articles, now reduced to 39, is approved by the Queen and Parliament.
1604	The Articles are added to English Canon Law.
1607	Jamestown established in Virginia.
1776	The American colonies declare their independence.
1789	The Articles are adopted in principle by the newly created American Episcopal Church.
1801	Articles are "established" by a special act of PECUSA's General Convention.
1979	The Articles are removed to the newly created "Historical Documents" section in the new *BCP*.
1988	The Articles are removed from the Constitution of PECUSA.

Bibliography

Avis, Paul. "What is 'Anglicanism?'," *The Study of Anglicanism*. eds. Stephen Sykes and John Booty. Philadelphia: Fortress Press, 1988.

Bainton, Roland. *The Reformation of the Sixteenth Century*. Boston: Beacon Press, 1985.

Bebbington, David. *Evangelicalism in Modern Britain*. Grand Rapids: Baker Books, 1989.

Bicknell, E. J. *A Theological Introduction to The Thirty-nine Articles of the Church of England, Third Edition*. London: Longmans, Green, & Co., 1955.

Boultbee, T. P. *A Commentary of The Thirty-nine Articles*. London: Longmans, Green, and Co., 1880.

Bradley, James, and Richard Muller, eds. *Church, Word, and Spirit*. Grand Rapids: Wm. Eerdmans, 1987.

Bromiley, Geoffrey. "Evangelism and the Anglican Articles 1563 - 1963," *Christianity Today* (March, 1963), 590.

-----. "A Curious Anniversary," *Christianity Today* (October, 1971), 5-7.

-----. "The English Protestant Creed," *Church, Word, and Spirit*. eds. James Bradley and Richard Muller. Grand Rapids: Wm. Eerdmans, 1981.

Brown, C. G. "Divided Loyalties? The Evangelicals, The Prayer-Book and The Articles," *Historical Magazine of the Protestant Episcopal Church, 44* (June, 1975), 189-209.

Browne, Edward Harold. *An Exposition of the Thirty-nine Articles*. New York: E.P. Dutton & Co., 1870.

Burnet, Gilbert. *An Exposition of the Thirty-nine Articles of the Church of England*. London: J. Walthoe, B. Tooke. Fourth Edition, 1720.

Cary, Henry. *Testimonies of the Fathers of the First Four Centuries to the Doctrine and Discipline of the Church of England as Set Forth in the Thirty-nine Articles*. Oxford: Talboys, 1835.

Chadwick, Owen. *The Reformation*. Middlesex: Pelican Books, 1972.

Comby, Jean. *How to Read Church History*, Vol. II. London: SCM Press, 1989.

Curtis, William A. *A History of Creeds and Confessions of Faith in Christendom and Beyond*. Edinburgh: T & T Clark, 1911.

de Toqueville, Alexis. *Democracy in America*, ed. Richard Heffner. New York: Penguin Books, 1984.

Dickens, A. G. *The English Reformation*. New York: Schocken Books, 1964.

Dugmore, C. W. "Foundation Documents of the Faith." *Expository Times, 91* (March, 1980), 164-167.

Duin, Julia. "Bishops Take a First Step." *United Voice, 5:2* (May 1992), 2.

Forbes, A. P. Bishop. *An Explanation of the Thirty-nine Articles.* London: E. P. Dutton & Co., 1867-1868.

Gaustad, Edwin. *A Documentary History of Religion in America: To the Civil War.* Grand Rapids: Eerdmans, 1982.

-----. *Faith of Our Fathers.* San Francisco: Harper & Row, 1987.

Gilbert, Bishop of Sarum. *An Exposition of the Thirty-nine Articles,* ed. James R. Page. New York: D. Appleton & Co., 1850.

Grammar, Carl. "The Meaning of the Thirty-nine Articles" No date, no publisher. Writer is identified as the "Rector of St. Stephen's Church, Philadelphia and sometime Professor of Church History and Canon Law at the Theological Seminary in Virginia.

Green, E. Tyrrell. *The Thirty-nine Articles and the Age of Reformation.* London: Wells Gardner, Darton & Co., nd.

Harmon, Nolan Bailey. "John Wesley and the Articles of Religion," *Religion in Life,* 22:2 (Spring, 1953), 290.

Hardwick, Charles. *A History of the Articles.* London: George Bell & Sons, 1895.

Hatch, Nathan. *The Democratization of American Christianity.* New Haven: Yale University Press, 1989.

Hatchett, Marion. *Commentary on the American Prayer Book.* New York: The Seabury Press, 1980.

Howe, John W. *Our Anglican Heritage.* Elgin: David C. Cook, 1977.

Hudson, Winthrop. *Religion in America.* New York: Charles Scribner's Sons, 1981.

Hylson-Smith, Kenneth. *Evangelicals in the Church of England: 1734-1984.* Edinburgh: T & T Clark, 1989.

Kidd, Richard Bentley Proson. *Testimonies and Authorities, Divine and Human, in Confirmation of the Thirty-nine Articles of The Church of England.* London: Cambridge, 1848.

Klaassen, Walter. *Anabaptism: Neither Catholic nor Protestant.* Waterloo, Ontario: Conrad Press, 1973.

Knox, David Broughton. "The Position of the Thirty-nine Articles in the Anglican Communion Today," *Reformed Theological Review, 30:8-13* (January - April, 1971).

-----. *Thirty-nine Articles: The Historic Basis of the Anglican Faith.* London: Hodder and Stoughton, 1967.

Lewis, C. S. *Mere Christianity.* New York: Macmillan, 1960.

Lloyd, Charles, ed. *Formularies of Faith Put Forth by Authority during The Reign of Henry VIII.* Oxford: Clarendon Press, 1825.

MacCulloch, Dairmaid. *Thomas Cranmer: A Life.* New Haven, CT: Yale University Press, 1996.

MacLear, G. F., and Williams, W. W. *An Introduction to the Thirty-nine Articles of the Church of England.* London: MacMillan and Co., 1895.

Martin, Marty. *Pilgrims in Their Own Land.* Boston: Little, Brown, & Co., 1984.

Miller, Kevin A. "Denominations Urged to Turn Focus 'Outward'." *Christianity Today* (October 3, 1994), 72.

Miller, V. C. *The Lambeth Articles.* Oxford: Latimer House, 1971.

Newman, John Henry. *History of My Religious Opinions.* London: Longman, Green, Longman, Roberts & Green, 1865.

-----. *Tract XC (90).* New York: H. B. Durrand, MDCCCLXV.

Noll, Mark. *Confessions and Catechisms of the Reformation.* Grand Rapids: Baker, 1991.

Norris, Richard. "Episcopacy," *The Study of Anglicanism,* eds. Stephen Sykes and John Booty. Philadelphia: Fortress Press, 1988.

Oakeley, Frederick. *The Subject of Tract XC Examined.* London: J. G. F. & J. Rivington, 1841.

O'Donovan, Oliver. *On the Thirty-nine Articles: A Conversation with Tudor Christianity.* Exeter: Pater Noster Press, 1981.

Packer, J. I. *A Guide to the 39 Articles Today.* London: Church Book Room Press, 1965.

-----. *The Thirty-nine Articles.* London: Falcon Books, 1961.

-----. *The Thirty-nine Articles, Their Place and Use Today.* Oxford: Latimer House, 1984.

Prichard, Robert. *A History of the Episcopal Church.* Harrisburg, Pennsylvania: Morehouse Publishing Co., 1991.

Rusticus. "Subscription No Bondage, or the Practical Advantages afforded by the Thirty-nine Articles in all the Branches of Academical Education," Oxford: J. H. Parker, 1835.

Ryle, John Charles. "The Thirty-nine Articles." An excerpt from his book *Knots Untied* published in 1877. London: Church Book Room Press, 1960.

Samuel, David, and George Carey. "The ARCIC Agreed Statements are not agreeable to Scripture and the Thirty-nine Articles of Religion," *The Churchman: Journal of Anglican Theology,* 10:2 (1988), 151-165.

Shepherd, Massey Hamilton. *The Oxford American Prayer Book Commentary.* New York: Oxford University Press, 1950.

-----. *The Worship of the Church.* Greenwich: Seabury Press, 1952.

Solheim, James. "Special Meeting of Bishops Expresses Determination to Make Radical Changes," *The Episcopal News Service* (March, 1992), 9.

Sperry, Earl Evelyn. "Why the Thirty-nine Articles Should be Retained," Philadelphia: The Evangelical Education Society of the Protestant Episcopal Church. Undated but from the introduction it is clear that it was written between 1925 and 1928.

Spencer, Bonnell. *Ye Are the Body.* Westpark, New York: Holy Cross Publishers, 1965.

Spitz, Lewis. *The Protestant Reformation.* New Jersey: Prentice Hall, Inc., 1966.

-----. *The Renaissance and Reformation Movements.* Vol. II. Chicago: Rand McNally & Co., 1972.

Starkey, Thomas. "An Exhortation to Unity and Obedience," *The Protestant Reformation.* New Jersey: Prentice Hall, 1966.

Steenson, Jeffrey. "Bishops Amend Sexualtiy Document" *The Living Church* (September 11, 1994), 9.

Stevenson, Taylor. "Lex Orandi — Lex Credendi," *The Study of Anglicanism.* eds. Stephen Sykes and John Booty. Philadelphia: Fortress Press, 1990.

"Report of the Archbishop's Commission on Christian Doctrine," *Subscription and Assent to the Thirty-nine Articles.* London: SPCK, 1968.

The Blue Book, Reports of the Committees, Commissions, Boards, and Agencies of the General Convention of the Episcopal Church. Detroit, 1988.

The Book of Common Prayer. New York: The Church Hymnal Corporation, 1979.

The Gallup Organization, Inc. "Report on The Spiritual Health of the Episcopal Church," Based on a survey conducted for The Episcopal Church Center, 1988.

The Oxford Dictionary of the Christian Church, (Revised) eds. F. L. Cross and E. A. Living Stone, Oxford: Oxford University Press, 1958.

Thomas, W. H. Griffith. *The Principles of Theology.* London: Vine Books, Ltd., 1978.

Toon, Peter. "The Articles and Homilies," *The Study of Anglicanism.* eds. Stephen Sykes and John Booty. Philadelphia: Fortress Press, 1988.

-----. "The English Protestant Creed," *Church, Word, and Spirit.* eds. James Bradley, and Richard Muller. Grand Rapids: Wm. Eerdmans, 1987.

Tuchman, Barbara. *The March of Folly: From Troy to Vietnam.* New York: Ballantine Books, 1984.

White, Edwin, and Jackson Dykman. *Annotated Constitution and Canons.* Vol 1. New York: Seabury Press, 1982.

Woolverton, John. *Colonial Anglicanism in North America.* Detroit: Wayne State University Press, 1984.

Wright, Tom. "Doctrine Declared," *Believing in the Church: The Corporate Nature of Faith A Report by the Doctrine Commission of the Church of England.* Wilton, Connecticut: Morehouse Barlow Co., 1981.

Zahl, Paul. *The Protestant Face of Anglicanism.* Grand Rapids: Eerdmans, 1998.